INTERACTIONS II
A Writing Process Book

SECOND EDITION

INTERACTIONS II
A Writing Process Book

Margaret Keenan Segal
Development Center for Afghan Education

Cheryl Pavlik
Oman Ministry of Education

With contributions by Jane Sturtevant,
Borough of Manhattan Community College,
and Laurie Blass

McGraw-Hill Publishing Company

New York St. Louis San Francisco Auckland Bogotá Caracas
Hamburg Lisbon London Madrid Mexico Milan
Montreal New Delhi Oklahoma City Paris San Juan
São Paulo Singapore Sydney Tokyo Toronto

This is an ⎡B⎤ book

Interactions II: A Writing Process Book
Second Edition

1 2 3 4 5 6 7 8 9 0   RMT RMT   9 5 4 3 2 1 0

ISBN 0-07-557540-X

Cover illustration: Frantisěk Kupka: *Lines, Planes, Depth,* c. 1920–22. Oil on canvas, 31½″ × 28½″. Albright-Knox Art Gallery, Buffalo, New York, Charles Clifton and George B. and Jenny R. Mathews Funds, 1977.

Sponsoring editor: Eirik Børve
Developmental editor: Mary McVey Gill
Project editor: Cathy de Heer
Production supervisor: Renée Reeves
Copyeditor: Stacey Sawyer
Proofreader: Karen Kevorkian
Illustrations: Sally Richardson
Photo research: Judy Mason
Interior and cover design: Cheryl Carrington
Composition: Graphic Typesetting Service
Color separation: Color Tech
Printing and binding: Rand McNally

CONTENTS

Chapter 3   BUSINESS AND MONEY   36

Rhetorical focus: persuasion (writing a letter to the editor)

Chapter 4   JOBS AND PROFESSIONS   50

Rhetorical focus: exposition (writing a personal description)

Chapter 9   THE SKY ABOVE US   124

Rhetorical focus: description (describing scientific topics)

Chapter 10   MEDICINE, MYTHS, AND MAGIC   140

Rhetorical focus: persuasion (writing about moral issues)

PREFACE
to the Second Edition

To the Instructor

INTERACTIONS: THE PROGRAM

Interactions consists of ten texts plus two instructor's manuals for in-college or college-bound nonnative English students. *Interactions I* is for high-beginning to low-intermediate students, while *Interactions II* is for low-intermediate to intermediate students. Within each level, I and II, the books are carefully coordinated by theme, vocabulary, grammar structure, and, where possible, language functions. A chapter in one book corresponds to and reinforces material taught in the same chapter of the other three books at that level for a truly integrated, four-skills approach.

   Each level, I and II, consists of five books plus an instructor's manual. In addition to *A Writing Process Book,* they include:

A Communicative Grammar I, II: Organized around grammatical topics, these books include notional/functional material where appropriate. They present all grammar in context and contain a wide variety of communicative activities.

A Reading Skills Book I, II: The selections in these books are written by the authors and carefully graded in level of difficulty and amount of vocabulary. They include many vocabulary-building exercises and emphasize reading strategies: for example, skimming, scanning, guessing meaning from context, understanding the structure and organization of a selection, increasing reading speed, and interpreting the author's point of view.

A Listening/Speaking Skills Book I, II: These books use lively, natural language from a variety of contexts—dialogues, interviews, lectures, and announcements. Listening strategies emphasized include summarizing main ideas, making inferences, and listening for stressed words, reductions, and intonation. A cassette tape program with instructor's key accompanies each text.

A Speaking Activities Book I, II: These books are designed to give students the opportunity to practice their speaking and listening skills in English by promoting realistic use of the language through individual, pair, and small-group work. Task-oriented and problem-solving activities simulate real-life situations and help develop fluency.

Instructor's Manual I, II: These manuals provide instructions and guidelines for use of the books separately or in any combination to form a program. For each of the core books except *Speaking Activities,* there is a separate section with teaching tips, additional activities, and other suggestions. The instructor's manual also includes sample tests for the grammars and readers.

The grammatical focus for the twelve chapters of *Interactions II* is as follows:

1. Review of basic verb tenses
2. Nouns, pronouns, and articles
3. Modal auxiliaries and related structures
4. The perfect tenses: *Would/used to, was/were going to*
5. Phrasal verbs and related structures
6. Compound and complex sentences; Clauses of time, condition, reason, contrast, and purpose
7. Transitions; The past perfect continuous tense
8. Adjectives and adverbs; Clauses and phrases of comparison
9. The passive voice
10. Adjective clauses
11. Common uses of infinitives, gerunds, and related structures
12. *Wish, hope,* and conditional sentences

INTERACTIONS II: A WRITING PROCESS BOOK

Rationale

Interactions II: A Writing Process Book was designed to lead students through the writing process and provide a variety of activities to help them master the wide array of writing skills necessary for academic writing. The text incorporates a number of features that set it apart from other writing books for nonnative students of English.

While most writing texts concentrate on the end product, *Interactions II: A Writing Process Book* shows students strategies that they can use in each step of the writing process.

The text consists of twelve chapters; each can be used for approximately four to six hours of classroom work. Each chapter is divided into twelve sections focusing on different steps in the writing process. These sections introduce various writing strategies and techniques and allow students to practice them one step at a time. This practice helps students understand how the different techniques work before they use them in their own writing. Students are given specific guidance in using their new skills to generate and organize ideas and to write, edit, and revise a paragraph or short composition of their own. At every step, students are encouraged to analyze and discuss the strategies they are employing. In this way, students focus on one skill at a time. Beginning students especially benefit from this step-by-step approach because they are usually more comfortable with structured practice. By the end of each chapter, students have acquired new skills and have produced their own paragraphs or compositions.

Appendices at the end of the book provide spelling, punctuation, and capitalization rules that students can use for reference. There are also feedback sheets for the instructor's use (see Teaching Suggestions).

Although the concept of writing as a process is central to the course, traditional areas of instruction such as paragraph form, mechanics, and grammar are practiced throughout. The emphasis, however, is on grammatical and lexical features that serve to unify a paragraph.

Since our own classroom experience shows that analyzing model paragraphs can be helpful and instructive, each chapter contains two or three tasks based on model paragraphs.

Chapter Organization

Exploring Ideas: The first problem that most students encounter is generating ideas. This section teaches strategies to help them with that task. Some of the methods presented are discussing and listing ideas, doing research, interviewing, ranking ideas, and free writing. A vocabulary-building activity provides students with some of the vocabulary they may need in writing their own paragraphs and encourages them to use fellow students and their teacher as resources for additional vocabulary development.

Organizing Ideas: In this section students are taught organizational skills such as writing effective topic and concluding sentences, ordering and limiting information in a paragraph, and organizing different types of compositions.

Developing Cohesion and Style: The focus of this section is on the grammatical and lexical features that serve to unify a paragraph. Students are taught the most natural use of structures and vocabulary in extended written discourse. Features such as transitional words, reference, varied word order, sequence of tenses, parallel construction, and structures that serve various rhetorical purposes are taught. Some sentence-level features that often cause students problems, such as choice of tense, are also covered in this section.

Writing the First Draft: Because most students do not realize that good writing is usually the product of many revisions, they are explicitly told that the first paragraph they write is only a draft.

Revising Your Writing: In this section students are given practice in revising for more global content and organizational problems before they edit for mechanical details. The development of ideas and the organization of paragraphs are stressed here.

Editing Practice: One of the most important skills for students to master is the ability to edit their work. This section provides them with paragraphs that contain common errors of form, grammar, spelling, punctuation, and capitalization. By finding errors in compositions they haven't written, students learn to critically evaluate their own writing with less anxiety. A positive approach to this step is recommended. Students should not be expected to find all errors, and working in small groups can make this activity more fun.

Editing Your Writing: After students practice editing, they are asked to edit their own compositions. Teachers can ask students to focus on specific aspects of their writing to make this step less frustrating. It is also suggested that students work with partners to help each other with this important step.

Writing the Second Draft: Only after students have had a chance to revise and edit their compositions are they required to hand in neatly written papers for the teacher's evaluation.

Sharing: Too often, students' interest in their writing ends when they receive a grade. This section provides ideas on how students can communicate with each other through their writing. Suggestions include using the writing as the basis of debate or discussion and creating class collections of compositions.

Using Feedback: This section enables students to use their teacher's feedback to help them evaluate their progress and take responsibility for improving their writing. At the end of the text, feedback sheets for each chapter are included. Teachers who wish to focus their feedback on the particular features covered in each chapter will find that these sheets make it easy to do so.

Developing Your Skills: This section provides additional reading and writing assignments to reinforce the chapter's teaching points and themes.

Developing Fluency: Unstructured journal writing assignments, both on and off the chapter topic, are featured here for extra writing practice.

Teaching Suggestions

The text has been designed for four hours of classwork per chapter, with homework assignments after each class, though some groups may require more classroom time. Although the text has a set format, it should not be considered prescriptive. More sophisticated students who may have already developed their own writing strategies should not be forced to abandon them. In addition, we recommend that you ask students to do as much extra free writing as possible; the instructor's manual contains suggestions for unstructured writing assignments.

Many tasks in the text are described as pair or group work. Though teachers should consider themselves free to adapt the tasks according to the needs and abilities of their own students, we feel that group and pair work helps students to develop self-confidence. Since writing is such a daunting task for most students, working with others may help them to see that all students have many of the same difficulties.

The feedback sheets at the end of the book are provided to help teachers organize their comments in a way that students can easily interpret. Teachers are encouraged to give as much positive feedback as possible, to focus on content before grammar, and to concentrate on the skills presented in each chapter. This approach is especially vital for beginning students, whose mistakes are so numerous.

Changes to the Second Edition

The second edition of *Interactions II: A Writing Process Book* remains dedicated to providing students with a variety of activities that guide them through the process of academic writing. In addition, however, each chapter includes many new features. These are:

■ More sentence-level language exercises
■ More writing assignments, both structured and free
■ Expanded editing exercises
■ Updated and expanded material on the chapter topic for students to discuss and write about
■ More contextualized vocabulary work
■ An expanded appendix
■ Many new photographs

Each chapter also includes two new sections, *Developing Your Skills* and *Developing Fluency*. *Developing Your Skills* gives students additional reading and writing assignments to reinforce the chapter's teaching points and themes. *Developing Fluency* provides students with unstructured writing assignments, both on and off the chapter topic.

ACKNOWLEDGMENTS

We would like to thank the many people who made these books possible: Mary McVey Gill, our editor, whose ideas, encouragement, and patience were invaluable; Cathy de Heer, responsible for taking the books through production; Stacey Sawyer, the copyeditor; and Sally Richardson, the artist, for bringing some of the characters to life. We would also like to thank the many educators who made us aware of the process of writing and the importance of discoursal features, and our students, the catalysts for all our ideas.

Also, thanks to the following reviewers of the first edition for their help in shaping the second edition: Robert Austin, Tacoma Community College; James Burke, El Paso Community College; Daniele J. Dibie, California State University at Northridge; David Fein, UCLA Extension; Marie Greco, Springfield Technical Community College; Matthew

Handelsman, St. Michael's College; Vivian Hefley, Iowa State University; Monica Kapadia, El Paso Community College; Martina Kusi-Mensah, Mountain View College, Dallas; Karen O'Neill, San Jose State University; Simin Rooholamini, County College of Morris; Lydia Samatar, Upsala College; Webster J. Van De Mark, Valencia Community College; and Ellen Wall, City College of San Francisco.

M. K. S.
C. P.

To the Student

Writing is like carrying things up steps. If you try to jump to the top with everything . . .

. . . you will have trouble.

If you carry small armfuls up step by step . . .

. . . you will reach the top.

STEPS TO WRITING

1. Exploring ideas
2. Organizing ideas
3. Developing cohesion and style
4. Writing the first draft
5. Revising your writing
6. Editing practice
7. Editing your writing
8. Writing the second draft
9. Sharing
10. Using feedback
11. Developing your skills
12. Developing fluency

TALKING ABOUT WRITING

Look at the steps to writing.

1. What do you do in each step?
2. Why is each step important?
3. Do you use these steps when you write in your language?
4. Which steps do you like to do? Why?
5. Which steps do you dislike?

Discuss how you write in your native language with other students in the class. Answer these questions:

1. How many times do you write and rewrite a paper?
2. Do you make an outline?
3. How do you think of ideas?
4. Do you talk to other people about what you write?
5. Do you check your paper for correct grammar, spelling, and punctuation?
6. Do you write in English the same way you write in your own language?

Look at these portions of first drafts of papers written by teachers and graduate students.

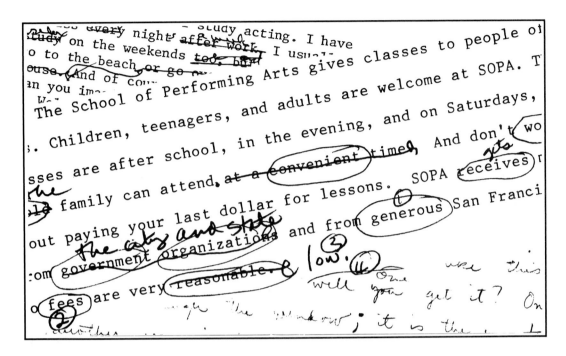

1. Do they write perfect papers the first time?
2. Do they change what they write?
3. Does your writing in your language look like these papers?
4. Now think about the pictures at the beginning of this preface. Why is writing like carrying things up steps?

M. K. S.
C. P.

INTERACTIONS II
A Writing Process Book

1

EDUCATION AND STUDENT LIFE

GETTING READY TO WRITE

Exploring Ideas

Before you write, think about what you want to say. In this section, you will learn ways to develop your ideas.

Ranking Things in Order of Importance

A. Here are some things an immigrant or a foreign student who is choosing a college might want to think about. Which ones are most important to you? Number them in order from 1 to 11, with 1 as the most important.

_____ class sizes

_____ facilities (libraries, laboratories)

_____ quality of ESL classes

_____ special programs for nonnative speakers

_____ courses offered

_____ location

_____ cost

_____ ease of admission

_____ prestige

_____ help with job placement

_____ friendliness of staff and students

A large college in a city

A small suburban college

B. Are there any other things you think are important? List them here.

_____

_____

_____

C. Discuss your lists with other students. Tell why you thought certain things were important.

Building Vocabulary

A. In your discussion you may have heard some words you don't understand, or you may have found that you didn't know the English word for some of the ideas you wanted to express. Ask the teacher the meaning of any words you don't understand and add them to the list below.

Nouns	Verbs	Adjectives	Other
advantage	attend	costly	
disadvantage	prefer	impersonal	_____
facility			
faculty	_____	_____	_____
location	_____	_____	_____
prestige			
	_____	_____	_____
_____	_____	_____	_____

B. With other students, discuss the advantages of large and small colleges. Consider some of the things in the list on page 2.

ADVANTAGES OF A LARGE COLLEGE

1. _____

2. _____

3. _____

4. _____

5. _____

6. _____

ADVANTAGES OF A SMALL COLLEGE

1. _____

2. _____

3. _____

4. _____

5. _____

6. _____

C. Look at your lists of advantages and discuss with other students whether large or small colleges are better for nonnative English-speaking students. Remember that some things may be more important than others.

D. Choose the topic you want to write about: the advantages of a large college or the advantages of a small college for immigrant or foreign students. Add to your list advantages other students mentioned that you think are important.

Organizing Ideas

Arranging Ideas in Order of Importance

Now that you have some ideas about your topic, you need to organize them. One way of doing this is to write about the most important ideas first, then the less important ones. Look at the list of advantages you made. Which advantages are most important? Number them in order of importance, with 1 as the most important.

Giving Reasons

When you write, you should give reasons for your opinions. List the advantages again in order of importance. Then give at least one reason for each of the advantages. This will make an outline you can use when you write.

Example: Advantage 1: Small schools have fewer students.
              Reason: It is easier to get to know the other students.

Advantage 1: _____

Reason: _____

Advantage 2: _____

Reason: _____

Advantage 3: _____

Reason: _____

Advantage 4: _____

Reason: _____

Advantage 5: _____

Reason: _____

Advantage 6: _____

Reason: _____

Writing Topic Sentences

> The topic sentence usually comes at the beginning of a paragraph. It tells the reader the main idea of the paragraph. A good topic sentence is neither too specific nor too general.

A. Here is a list of possible topic sentences for a different paragraph about the advantages of studying abroad. Discuss them in groups or as a class. Are any topic sentences too specific or too general? Your classmates may have several different opinions, and there is no one correct answer.

1. Students who study abroad often can't speak the language well.
2. Studying abroad has three main advantages.
3. There are several reasons why students should study abroad.
4. There are many good schools in foreign countries.
5. If possible, all college students should spend some time studying in a foreign country.

An English class for foreign students

B. Write a topic sentence for your paragraph about the advantages of large or small colleges. It can be similar to one of the topic sentences above.

_____

_____

C. Have another student read your topic sentence and discuss how you might improve it. Read the other student's topic sentence. Answer the questions on the next page.

1. Is it a complete sentence?
2. Does it tell the reader what you are going to write about?
3. Is it too general or too specific?

A foreign student and her advisor

PART TWO
DEVELOPING WRITING SKILLS
Developing Cohesion and Style

Developing your ideas and organization is very important; however, you must also learn to use English structures effectively and correctly. In this section you will practice some of the structures that will help you to unify your paragraph—make it more *cohesive*. You will also learn how to make your writing sound more natural.

Giving Reasons: *Because, So, Therefore*

When you give reasons for your ideas, you may want to use connectors that show cause or result.

Because appears in phrases and clauses that state a cause (a reason).

Examples: *Because* large schools offer many different courses, students have a wide choice of subjects to take.

Students have a wide choice of subjects to take *because* large schools offer many different courses.

> *So* and *therefore* appear in phrases and clauses that state a result.
>
> *Examples:* Large schools offer many different courses. *Therefore,* students
> have a wide choice of subjects to take.
>
> Large schools offer many different courses, *so* students have a wide
> choice of subjects to take.

Complete the following sentences with *because, so,* or *therefore.* Note the different punctuation and capitalization in sentences with these three connectors.

1. Students who study in a foreign country live with people who do not speak their native language; _____, they will learn a foreign language well.
2. Public colleges in your own state are more practical _____ they are less expensive.
3. When students attend a local college, they can live at home _____ they don't have to spend a lot on rent and food.
4. _____ students have to study in a foreign language, they often have difficulty with their courses.
5. Foreign students spend a long time away from home. _____, they may forget their own customs and culture.

Using Transition Words: *In Addition, Also*

> When you write a paragraph that lists information, you must use transition words—words that connect your ideas. If you don't use transition words, your paragraph will sound "choppy"—that is, not cohesive.

A. Read the following paragraph.

Why Study Abroad?

Studying abroad offers students many advantages. The students live in a new culture, so they can learn both in and out of the classroom. They learn to be flexible, because they have to adapt to different ways of living. They are far from home. Therefore, they have to become responsible and self-reliant. They have an experience they will remember all their lives.

A writer can make a paragraph more cohesive by adding the transitions *also* and *in addition*.

Examples: It is very difficult to study abroad. *In addition,* it can be much more expensive than studying in your own country.

It is very difficult to study abroad. *Also,* it can be much more expensive than studying in your own country.

In addition usually comes at the beginning of a sentence. In this position, it always takes a comma.

Also can come at the beginning of a sentence, before a simple present or a past tense verb, or after an auxiliary verb or a modal. If it comes at the beginning, a comma always follows it.

B. Rewrite the second example above, putting *also* after the first auxiliary verb.

_____

_____

C. Use the transition words *in addition* or *also* to connect these pairs of ideas.

1. Undergraduate students are usually too immature to live away from home. They are too irresponsible.

   _____

   _____

2. Most students in four-year colleges are very intelligent. They study hard.

   _____

   _____

3. Professors in small colleges don't understand foreign students. They may know very little about foreign cultures.

   _____

   _____

4. Students who go abroad to study lose contact with their families. Many of them marry foreigners and never return home.

   _____

   _____

Using Transition Words: *First of All, Finally*

> Two other useful transitions are *first of all* and *finally.*

A. Read this paragraph. Note that *first of all* and *finally* always come at the beginning of a sentence and always take a comma.

> There are several reasons that undergraduate students should not study away from home. *First of all,* living away from home is much more expensive than living at home. In addition, most teenagers are not mature enough to live far away from their families. Therefore, they often get into trouble. Also, many students feel lonely and homesick, so they are unable to study. *Finally,* many students who go away to study never return to their countries.

B. Rewrite the paragraph above, using the transitions *in addition, also, first of all,* and *finally.* Remember to use commas where necessary.

Moderating Opinions: Adverbs of Frequency and Quantifiers

> When you state an opinion, you usually moderate it (make it less strong) with an adverb of frequency (such as *usually* or *often*) or a quantifier (such as *some* or *many*). Also, be careful when you use a noun with no modifier. For example, in the sentence *Foreign students work harder than native English speakers,* it is important to add *many* or *most* or *some* before the subject, *foreign students.*

What are the problems with the sentences that follow?

All foreign students have a difficult time their first year.
Foreign students never become friendly with Americans.
No foreign student gets better grades than native English-speaking students.

> You can easily substitute other adverbs of frequency for *never* or *always* and other quantifiers for *all* or *no.*
>
> 1.   Instead of *never,* use *rarely, almost never, hardly ever,* or *usually . . . not.*
>
>   *Example:*   Teachers never have time to discuss a student's personal problems.
>   *Correction:*   Teachers usually don't have time to discuss a student's personal problems.

2. Instead of *always,* use *usually, almost always,* or *often.*

   Example: First-year students always have roommate problems.
   Correction: First-year students often have roommate problems.

3. Instead of *all,* use *almost all, almost every, most,* or *many.*

   Example: All foreign students get homesick.
   Correction: Almost every foreign student gets homesick.

4. Instead of *no* or *none,* use *very few, hardly any, almost no,* or *almost none.*

   Example: No foreign student learns English easily.
   Correction: Very few foreign students learn English easily.

Substitute or add words and phrases to moderate these statements.

1. Students in city colleges are too busy to be friendly.

   _____

   _____

2. Four-year colleges don't offer practical training.

   _____

   _____

3. Studying in a foreign language is always very difficult.

   _____

   _____

© ALAN KAREY/IMAGE WORKS

4. All students in community colleges* can live at home.

    _____

    _____

5. Studying in a private college is extremely expensive.

    _____

    _____

Writing the First Draft

> You have developed and organized your ideas and thought about the way you will write them. Now you are ready to write your paragraph. However, the paragraph you write will still need work; we call this paragraph a *draft*. A draft is an intermediate step, not the final product.

Write the first draft of your paragraph on the advantages of large or small colleges. Remember to include reasons for all of your opinions and to use transition words to connect your ideas. Write on every other line, so that it will be easy to make changes in your paragraph.

PART THREE

REVISING AND EDITING

Revising Your Writing

Adding Reasons to a Paragraph

> After you write the first draft of your paragraph, reread it carefully. When you first reread it, do not try to find problems with grammar, punctuation, form, or spelling. Look for problems in the content and organization of the paragraph. For example:
>
> 1. Content
>   a. Did you include everything that you wanted to say?
>   b. Did you give a reason for each opinion?

---

*A community college is a two-year college. Community colleges usually offer programs in secretarial, technical, health-care, and other job-related skills.

2. Organization

   a. Does your topic sentence give the main idea of your paragraph?
   b. Did you organize your ideas from most important to least important?

3. Cohesion and style

   a. Did you use transition words and connectors?
   b. Did you use adverbs of frequency and quantifiers?

A. Read the following paragraph. What problems can you find in it?

Studying in a community college has several advantages. Most community colleges teach job skills. Many community college programs are ideal for part-time students. Community colleges are usually less expensive than four-year colleges. Students can live at home.

Students at a community college

B. You can see that the writer of the preceding paragraph listed what he or she thinks are the advantages of studying in a community college but did not include reasons. Rewrite the paragraph, inserting the reasons below. Use the words *so, because,* and *therefore.* Add the transition words *also, in addition, first of all,* and *finally* where appropriate.

REASONS

Students can work and go to school too.
Students with low incomes can afford them.
Students can easily find a job after graduation.
Students don't have to pay for room and board.

C. Revise the first draft of your paragraph on the advantages of large (small) colleges. Then show it to another student. Can he or she find any problem in its content?

Editing Practice

After you revise your paragraph for content, you should edit it. When you edit, look for problems in grammar, punctuation, form, and spelling.

Using Correct Paragraph Format

Here are some rules about the correct form of a paragraph. (For more rules on capitalization and punctuation, see the appendix at the end of this book.)

1. Always indent the first sentence of your paragraph.
2. Leave a left and right margin.
3. Begin each sentence with a capital letter.
4. End each sentence with a period (.), a question mark (?), or an exclamation mark (!).
5. Make sure that the end punctuation immediately follows the last word of the sentence.
6. Leave a small space between sentences. (On a typewriter, leave two spaces.)
7. Divide words between syllables. (A dictionary will tell you where to divide a word if you aren't sure where the syllables begin and end.)
8. Never divide one-syllable words.

The writer of the following paragraph broke each of the eight preceding rules at least once. Rewrite the paragraph and correct the mistakes. Then check your paragraph against the paragraph on page 10.

> There are several reasons that undergraduate students sh-
> ould not study away from home first of all, living away from
> home is much more expensive than living at home In additi-
> on, most teenagers are not mature enough to live far away
> from their families . Therefore, they often get into trou
> ble.many students feel very lonely and homesick
>   So they are not able to study.

Making General Statements with Present-Tense Verbs

In English, there are several ways to make statements that are generally true. Look at the sentences in the exercises in this unit and answer these questions:

1. What tense are the verbs?
2. Are the subjects usually singular or plural?
3. Does the article *the* usually precede the subjects?

You will notice that general statement are in the simple present tense and that the subjects are usually plural with no articles. When the subjects are people, singular personal pronouns can be awkward in English. For example, look at these sentences. Which sentence sounds more awkward? Why?

> Students must leave their families.
>
> A student must leave his or her family.

When you are editing compositions that contain general statements, make sure that you follow these rules:

1. Use simple present verbs.
2. Add *-s* to verbs with third-person singular subjects (*he, she,* or *it*).
3. Count nouns should generally be plural with no article. (You will see more on the use of noncount nouns in Chapter 2.)
4. Pronouns must agree in number with their antecedents. *Every student should keep his or her culture* is correct although it is awkward. *Every student should keep their culture* would be wrong because *student* is singular.

The underlined words in these sentences may be wrong. Edit the sentences according to the preceding four rules, changing the words that are incorrect. Some sentences are correct.

1. Most <u>family save</u> for many years to send <u>his</u> children to college.

2. Students <u>feel</u> homesick.

3. <u>Small schools</u> don't have good <u>library.</u>

4. A large school has many students in <u>their</u> classes.

5. A school with many students <u>aren't</u> very friendly.

6. <u>People</u> who work can easily attend community colleges.

Editing Your Writing

Edit the paragraph you wrote. You can also give it to a partner to check. Use this checklist.

GRAMMAR
1. Present-tense verbs
2. Subject–verb agreement (*verb* + *s* with singular subjects)
3. Pronoun–antecedent agreement
4. No articles with plural count nouns (in a few cases, singular nouns with articles are correct)

FORM
1. Paragraph form (indentation, capitalization, division of words between syllables, punctuation, margins)
2. Spelling

Writing the Second Draft

After you edit your paragraph, rewrite it neatly, using good handwriting and correct form.

PART FOUR

COMMUNICATING THROUGH WRITING

Sharing

Give your second draft to your teacher for comments.

> The purpose of writing is to communicate a message. This section will give you ideas on how to use your writing as real communication.

Since the paragraphs the class wrote for this chapter gave opinions, you can use them for a debate. Divide the class into two groups: students who think that small colleges are better for foreign students and students who prefer large colleges. First meet with the members of your team and read one another's compositions. Make a list of your arguments. Then try to guess what the other team will argue and think of reasons against their arguments. (These are called *rebuttals*.)

Choose three students to represent each side. One will give the arguments (about five minutes), one the rebuttal (about three minutes), and one the summary (about three minutes).

Using Feedback

> The feedback you receive from your teacher can be a very valuable tool in helping you improve your writing. If you don't understand something about your teacher's comments, ask about it. Then answer these questions about your writing:
>
> 1. What do I do best?
> 2. What are my biggest problems?
> 3. Which of these problems are the result of carelessness? Not understanding how to write?
> 4. What can I do to help solve these problems?

Developing Your Skills

A. Write another paragraph about the advantages or disadvantages of one of the following topics (or choose your own topic).

1. small towns / large cities
2. bilingual education / monolingual education
3. city colleges / colleges in the country
4. small families / large families
5. an arts degree / a science degree
6. life today / life in the past

B. Look through some magazines and read the advertisements. Choose an ad that shows a product's advantages. Make a list of all the advantages it describes. Give your list and the picture without the text to a partner. See if he or she can write the text using your list. Then compare your partner's ad with the real ad. How are they different? How are they the same?

Developing Fluency

A. Start to keep a journal. In this journal, write whatever ideas come into your head. Your teacher can ask you to write in your journal in class or at home. Don't worry about grammar or correct form. Concentrate on ideas. Start now and write for ten minutes about anything you want. If you can't think of anything to say, write about how you can't think of anything.

B. Write in your journal about your school and/or your English class. What do you like about it? What do you dislike? What do you find difficult? What is easy for you?

2

CITY LIFE

GETTING READY TO WRITE

Exploring Ideas

Describing Scenes

A. Look at these pictures of city streets and choose one of them to describe. Write as much as you can in ten minutes. You can answer some of these questions.

1. What kind of street is this?
2. What is happening on the street?
3. What kinds of people live on this street?
4. How do you feel about the street?
5. How is the street similar to or different from the street where you live?

© BARBARA RIOS/PHOTO RESEARCHERS

© PHOTO RESEARCHERS

B. Discuss what you wrote with a few other students who wrote about the same picture. Did you notice the same things in the picture? Did you feel the same way about the street?

Including Sense Details and Feelings

In this chapter, you are going to write a personal description of the place where you live. You can describe your neighborhood, your street, your dorm, your apartment or house, or your room. A good description includes *sense details:* the things you can see, hear, touch, taste, and smell.

A. Write the name of the place you are going to describe here (for instance, "My Neighborhood"):

_____

B. Make a list of sense details.

  1. What I can see: _____

     _____

     _____

  2. What I can hear: _____

     _____

     _____

  3. What I can touch: _____

     _____

     _____

  4. What I can taste (optional): _____

     _____

     _____

  5. What I can smell (optional): _____

     _____

     _____

C. A *personal* description also includes the feelings and opinions the writer has about the place he or she is describing. Write a few notes about *how* you feel about the place you describe. Also write about *why* you feel the way you do.

_____

_____

_____

_____

D. Describe the place you chose to a partner. Ask each other questions about the places you describe.

Building Vocabulary

> If you use specific descriptive words, you can make your paragraph more interesting.

A. Read the following paragraph. The descriptive words and phrases are underlined. Discuss the meanings of unfamiliar items and tell which sense they describe.

My Neighborhood

Since people from all over the world live in my neighborhood, it is a fascinating place to explore. When I walk down the main street of the neighborhood, I can hear the <u>babble</u> of languages from all over the globe. Each language is accompanied by a <u>colorful ethnic shop</u> or <u>exotic restaurant.</u> On a <u>warm</u> evening I can smell the <u>sweet</u> melons from the Korean produce store or the <u>aroma of newly baked bread</u> from the Hungarian bakery. These smells are free, but for a small price I can also buy any of fifty kinds of <u>cheeses with unpronounceable names</u> from one store or <u>strange Asian vegetables</u> and the <u>spices to liven them up</u> from another. The people of the neighborhood take pride in their surroundings. They build <u>neighborhood churches, synagogues, and clubs in all different architectural styles.</u> On almost every street they plant <u>trees and flowers from their native countries</u> to remind them of home and to <u>brighten up</u> the <u>dreary gray</u> cement and <u>run-down</u> apartment buildings. One neighbor of mine plants <u>delicate Scottish flowers</u> every year in memory of her mother's garden in Scotland. Another neighbor has a <u>Chinese vegetable garden in window boxes.</u> I don't need to buy an airplane ticket to experience the world; a walk around my neighborhood can be just as exciting.

© CHARLES HARBUTT/ARCHIVE PICTURES

© CHARLES HARBUTT/ARCHIVE PICTURES

B. Choose one of these pictures. In small groups, make lists of words that describe the neighborhood. Then use those words to describe the picture.

1. What you can see: _____

   _____

2. What you can hear: _____

   _____

3. What you can smell: _____

   _____

4.   What you can taste: _____

_____

5.   What you can feel: _____

_____

Organizing Ideas

Writing Topic Sentences

> The topic sentence gives the main idea of a paragraph. It is often the first sentence in the paragraph and should express an idea you can easily write about in one paragraph. The topic sentence should not be too general. If it is, there will be too much to write about, and you will need more than one paragraph.
>
> Also, a good topic sentence should have a clear *focus*. This means it should present a *particular* idea, feeling, or opinion about the topic.
>
> *Too general:*   My neighborhood is a nice place to live.
>
> *A good topic sentence:*   My neighborhood is fascinating because people from many countries live in it.

A.   In each pair of topic sentences below, identify the one sentence that is too general and the one that has a clear focus.

1.   Topic: "My Room"

   a.   My room is a perfect place for one person to live.

   b.   Many people live in single rooms.

2.   Topic: "My House"

   a.   I love my house because it is filled with happy memories.

   b.   There are a lot of houses like mine in my neighborhood.

3.   Topic: "My Dormitory"

   a.   My dormitory has never felt like home to me.

   b.   I live in a dormitory.

B.   Write a topic sentence for your own paragraph. Then someone should write a few of the topic sentences from the class on the board. Discuss them as a class. Are any of them too general? Do they express a particular feeling or an opinion about the topic?

_____

_____

Adding Details to a Paragraph

The other sentences in the paragraph should develop the idea in the topic sentence. Look at the details that the writer is going to use to develop this topic sentence.

Topic sentence: My neighborhood is fascinating because people from many countries live in it.

- great shops—German butcher shop, Hungarian bakery, Czechoslovakian handicrafts and food shop, French cheese store
- the food from the shops smells good
- ethnic restaurants
- hear many different languages
- woman next door plants flowers to remind her of Scotland
- beautiful churches and synagogues

© KATRIN THOMAS/PHOTO RESEARCHERS

A Ukrainian shop in New York City

Make notes you could use for sentences to develop your topic sentence. These notes are just ideas for you to think about. You don't have to use all the notes you make, and when you are writing your paragraph you may think of other ideas to write about. For now just write some ideas down on paper.

Checking That All the Details Develop the Topic Sentence

> All the details in the paragraph should develop the idea given in the topic sentence. They should be on the topic.

A. In the following list, one detail is not on the topic. Which one is it? Cross it out.

> *Topic sentence:*   My room is small, but it is very cozy and has everything I need.

- is small but has enough space for my things, with a big closet
- has a big window with a view of a beautiful oak tree where there are often birds and squirrels
- landlord is not very pleasant
- is on the second floor and is quiet
- is nice and warm in winter
- has a small refrigerator and a cabinet for dishes

B. Look at the details you wrote for your paragraph and show them to a partner. Add any others you can think of and cross out the ones that are not on the topic.

Writing Concluding Sentences

> Most paragraphs have concluding sentences, which may repeat the idea of the topic sentence in different words or give a personal reaction to the topic of the paragraph. Here is a concluding sentence for the ideas about the ethnic neighborhood.
>
> I don't need to buy an airplane ticket to experience the world; a walk around my neighborhood is just as exciting.
>
> Here is a good concluding sentence for a paragraph about how a Brazilian student felt about living in a dorm with no other students from Brazil.
>
> Although I often felt lonely and homesick at first, I feel that I made some good American friends because I didn't have people from Brazil to talk with.

Give examples of some possible concluding sentences for these topics.

1. living in an apartment with two sloppy roommates

_____

_____

2. living in a run-down neighborhood where there's a lot of crime

_____

_____

3. living with your family

_____

_____

4. living in an old house

_____

_____

5. living in a small room in a modern dorm

_____

_____

PART TWO

DEVELOPING WRITING SKILLS

Developing Cohesion and Style

Giving Reasons: *Since*

Because and *since* have almost the same meaning. *Since* is very common in writing. Look at the following examples of sentences with *since*. Why does the first sentence have a comma?

Examples: *Since* quite a few people in the neighborhood come from Germany, there are many great German shops and restaurants here.

There are many great German shops and restaurants here *since* quite a few people in the neighborhood come from Germany.

Combine these sentences using *since*. The clause with *since* can come at the beginning or the end of the sentence. Use a comma after the clause if you put it at the beginning of the sentence.

1. Many people have lived in my neighborhood for years. It is a very friendly place.

_____

_____

2. My apartment is small. I have to keep it very neat.

_____

_____

3. My street is often dirty and smells like garbage. Many food stores are on it.

_____

_____

4. It is easy to get to know everyone in my dorm. Only forty people live in it.

_____

_____

Varying Word Order

If most of the sentences in a paragraph begin the same way, the paragraph may be boring. For example:

My neighborhood is fascinating because people from all over the world live in it. They speak many different languages. They take pride in the neighborhood. They plant flowers that remind them of their country. They build beautiful churches....

You can make the paragraph sound better if you begin some of the sentences with dependent clauses (beginning with words such as *because, since, when,* and *before*) or prepositional phrases (beginning with words such as *in, on, from,* and *with*). Which sentences in the paragraph on page 21 begin with dependent clauses or prepositional phrases? Note that a comma generally follows a beginning clause or phrase that is more than five words long.

International products are available at this grocery store in Manhattan, New York.

Writing the First Draft

Write your paragraph using the topic sentence you wrote and the notes you made. Make your paragraph interesting by adding details. Don't worry about grammar when you write the first draft. Write on every other line so you can revise your paragraph.

PART THREE

REVISING AND EDITING

Revising Your Writing

Revising with the Topic Sentence in Mind

After you write the first draft you should revise it. First read it to see if you like it. Add some interesting details if you want. Cross out the parts you think aren't very interesting.

Then read your paragraph again. Do all of your sentences develop the idea in your topic sentence? If they don't, there are two things you can do:

1. Maybe you started to write about an idea that is different from the idea in your topic sentence. If you like the idea, you should change your topic sentence.
2. Maybe some of your sentences are not about the idea in your topic sentence. You should cross out those sentences.

A. Look at the following two paragraphs. Should the writer change the topic sentence or cross out some sentences? Correct the paragraphs according to your decision about each. There may be several correct ways to revise these paragraphs.

I live in an ordinary house on an ordinary street in an ordinary suburb, and I think it is terrific! My house is now about thirty years old, but it looks newer. I used to live in a small apartment, first in Florida, and then in New Mexico. It is like hundreds of other houses in the suburbs, one story with an attached garage. There is nothing special about the house, and it won't win any prizes for architecture, but it's perfect for my family. The kitchen is big and has new appliances, including a washing machine and dryer. I hate the heat, but we have air conditioning in the living room and bedrooms, so it is always cool. I don't know why some Americans I know don't like the suburbs. For the kids there's a nice yard where they can play. I am very thankful that we can afford this house and live our ordinary lives in it.

When I came from Syria five years ago, I moved into my uncle's house in a suburb of Detroit. It is a small house with a tree-filled yard. My house in Syria was big, but many people lived in it. It was an old clay house with a roof that used to leak the few times it rained. We had a small courtyard with a fountain in it, and around the courtyard were all the rooms of the house. Because the climate in Syria is hot and dry, we appreciated the cool fountain and the plants and flowers in the courtyard. The house was never lonely, because my six brothers and sisters, my brother's wife and children, and my aunt's children all shared it. We didn't have a lot of furniture or appliances, but my mother and aunt made wonderful meals without any fancy equipment. I was very happy in that house, and I miss it now.

B. Revise the paragraph you wrote. Check for the following items when you revise.

1. Content

   Can you add descriptive details to make the paragraph more interesting?

2. Organization

   a. Should you change your topic sentence because it doesn't give the main idea of your paragraph?
   b. Should you cross out any details that don't develop the idea in the topic sentence?
   c. Do you have a concluding sentence that gives your feelings?

3. Cohesion and style

   a. Have you given reasons for your feelings?
   b. Have you varied the word order of your sentences?

Editing Practice

Correcting Run-on Sentences

A run-on sentence is an incorrect sentence made of two independent sentences connected with a comma.

Run-on: I am living in a dorm room, it is much too small for my roommate and me.

Run-on: First you notice all the exciting sights, later you notice the dirt.

You can correct a run-on sentence in two ways.

1. Change the comma to a period or a semicolon.

   I am living in a dorm room. It is much too small for my roommate and me.

   First you notice all the exciting sights; later you notice the dirt.

2. Change the run-on sentence into a sentence with two clauses. This often makes the sentence smoother and easier to read.

   I am living in a dorm room that is much too small for my roommate and me.

   First you notice all the exciting sights, and later you notice the dirt.

   The following words often begin new sentences, but students sometimes use them after commas in run-on sentences. Check for them when you edit.

it	he	she	they	then	however	therefore	later

A. Correct these run-on sentences.

1. My suburban apartment is big and sunny, it has a living room with large windows filled with plants.

2. I have a roommate who is very sloppy, she never washes the dishes, and she leaves her clothes all over the apartment.

3. I like my street because my neighbors are wonderful, they will help anybody who is having problems.

4. I fixed up my room this fall. First I painted it a pale blue, later I made new curtains.

5. My favorite place to relax is the park up the hill from my apartment, it is a steep climb, therefore it is rarely crowded.

6. My street is dirty and noisy, however it is filled with life and everyone on it is friendly.

B. Edit this paragraph for run-on sentences and rewrite it correctly.

My neighborhood is a fascinating place, it is in one of the biggest cities in the world, New York City, however, there is a small-town feeling to it. Most of the buildings in the neighborhood are small brick apartment houses with peeling red and brown paint. Many of the people here have lived in the neighborhood for years, they know each other and take pride in the neighborhood. They have planted trees and flowers in front of the buildings, they have built benches where the old people sit and talk. Since many of the people are from Germany and Eastern Europe, there are wonderful German, Hungarian, and Czechoslovakian shops here. I wouldn't want to live in any other neighborhood of the city.

Using Noncount Nouns

Many nouns in English are always singular because they are *noncount*—you can't count them. Which of these nouns are noncount (normally aren't plural)?

bakery	cement	pride	village
bread	neighborhood	lettuce	world

Nouns that are countable in some languages may be noncount nouns in English. Check the chart in the appendix in the back of the book for a list of common noncount nouns. When you edit your paragraph, check it to see if you have used noncount nouns correctly.

Editing Your Writing

Edit the paragraph you wrote. You can also give it to a partner to check. Use this checklist.

GRAMMAR

1. No run-on sentences
2. Verb forms and tenses
3. Noncount and count nouns

FORM

1. Indentation of the first word of each paragraph
2. Margins
3. Capital letters at the beginning of sentences
4. Division of words between syllables
5. Spelling
6. Neat handwriting

Writing the Second Draft

After you edit your paragraph, rewrite it neatly, using good handwriting and correct form.

PART FOUR

COMMUNICATING THROUGH WRITING

Sharing

Give your paragraph to your teacher for comments.

Read your paragraph without its topic sentence. The other students can suggest some good topic sentences for it. Did anyone suggest a sentence that was similar to yours?

Using Feedback

When your teacher returns your corrected paragraph, look at the comments carefully. If you don't understand something, ask about it. Then make a list of things you should check more carefully when you revise and edit.

Developing Your Skills

A. Look at the paragraphs in a description of your school (from a brochure or a school catalog) or in a selection you use for reading. Try to find the topic sentence of each paragraph. Did some topic sentences come in the middle or the end of the paragraph? How many paragraphs had no topic sentences?

B. Find other descriptions of people, places, or things. Which descriptions are personal (including feelings and opinions)? Which descriptions are impersonal (including facts, not feelings)? Did the writer use sense details? If so, how?

C. Write a description of your school. Use a process similar to the one you used in this chapter. Some students can write a personal description, like something you would write in a letter to a friend. Others can write an impersonal description, like something for a brochure about the school. Compare your descriptions.

Developing Fluency

A. Write two descriptions of a person you know. Write each description in ten minutes. Make the first impersonal, including only facts. Make the second personal, including feelings and opinions.

B. Describe a common object—for example, a pencil, a brick wall, or a telephone. Don't write the name of the object, but include as many details as possible in the description. Read your descriptions to the class. Can your classmates guess what you are describing?

C. Chose a topic you would like your partner to write about in his or her journal. Write about the topic your partner chooses for you.

3

BUSINESS AND MONEY

GETTING READY TO WRITE

Exploring Ideas

Discussing Attitudes Toward Money

A. Read these famous quotations and proverbs about money. In small groups, discuss the sayings. Do you agree with them or not? What attitude toward money does each one express?

> If possible, make money honestly; if not, make it by any means.
> —Horace (65–8 B.C.)

> If you would know the value of money, go and try to borrow some; for he that goes a-borrowing goes sorrowing. —Benjamin Franklin (1706–1790)

Time is money. —Benjamin Franklin (1706–1790)

Money is indeed the most important thing in the world; and all sound and successful personal and national morality should have this fact for its basis. —George Bernard Shaw (1856–1950)

Money speaks sense in a language all nations understand.
    —Aphra Behn (1640–1689)

And money is like muck, not good except it be spread.
    —Francis Bacon (1561–1626)

Money is our madness, our vast collective madness.
    —D. H. Lawrence (1885–1930)

It has been said that the love of money is the root of all evil. The want of money is so quite as truly. —Samuel Butler (1835–1902)

B. Translate a quotation or a proverb about money from your own language into English. Discuss the quotations. What attitudes toward money do they show?

C. Write as much as you can in ten minutes about your own attitude toward money.

D. Read this newspaper article and discuss the different people's reactions to the event it describes. You are going to write a letter to the editor in response to it.

Luck or Thievery?

COLUMBUS, OHIO. October 28 was a lucky day for motorists driving along Interstate 71 at about 9:30 in the morning. As a truck from the Metropolitan Armored Car Company sped down the highway, its back door blew open, spilling bags of money onto the road. When other vehicles hit the bags, they split open, spewing out a million dollars.

It didn't take motorists long to realize that the paper swirling around them was hard cash. They stopped on and around the highway and scooped up handfuls of money, gleefully cramming $20, $50, $100, even $1,000 dollar bills into bags, pockets, and purses. When the police arrived, they estimated that two hundred people were helping themselves to this bonanza.

Officials hoping to recover this money were not so gleeful. Columbus Mayor Dana G. Rinehart called these people thieves and said, "May they have many sleepless nights." He claims the government will prosecute anyone the police can find.

To encourage the return of the money, Metropolitan Armored Car has offered a reward of 10% percent of all the money they receive. So far, however, they have received only $100,000—from about thirty different people. One man turned in $57,000. Another man, however, called to say he was set for life and was leaving town. Since the cash was insured and belonged to local banks, many people can't see that they are hurting real people by keeping it.

Even if the government prosecutes, it will have trouble convicting the thieves. "Probably two-thirds of the jurors would think the defendant should have kept the money," said prosecutor Michael Miller.

—Adapted from "Luck or Thievery?" *Herald Tribune International Edition*, October 28, 1987

Building Vocabulary

A. You can guess the meanings of many of the new words in the newspaper article from context. Match these vocabulary words with their meanings.

1. ___ armored	a.	very happy		
2. ___ split	b.	pick up		
3. ___ spew	c.	charge with a crime		
4. ___ swirl	d.	tear open		
5. ___ scoop up	e.	move in circles		
6. ___ gleeful	f.	spill		
7. ___ bonanza	g.	something of great value		
8. ___ prosecute	h.	protected with strong metal		
9. ___ convict	i.	find guilty		

B. In your response, you might want to use some of the words that you weren't familiar with. First categorize them into parts of speech. Then make sentences with six of the words, giving your opinion of the happenings in the article.

Nouns	Verbs	Adjectives
		armored

Example: Maybe the drivers of the *armored* car didn't lock the doors intentionally.

Organizing Ideas

Writing Reactions to a Reading Selection

A. Discuss these questions in small groups.

1. Is it wrong to keep money that you haven't earned?
2. What does it mean that the money is *insured*? Who will pay back the money? Is it true that the loss of the money doesn't hurt anyone?
3. What would you do if you were one of the motorists? Would you take the money? What would you do if you were an official of the town?

B. Should the motorists return the money? Write reasons why or why not below and on the next page.

REASONS WHY THE MOTORISTS SHOULD RETURN THE MONEY

_____

_____

_____

_____

_____

REASONS WHY THE MOTORISTS SHOULD NOT RETURN THE MONEY

_____

_____

_____

_____

C. Read what you wrote about your attitude toward money in the "Exploring Ideas" section. Do you think the motorists should or should not return the money? Does your attitude toward money support your opinion?

Analyzing the Organization of a Letter to the Editor

A. Read this letter to the editor of a newspaper.

Home Free

Regarding the report on Americans who don't pay taxes on money they make from small home businesses (Oct. 23): My opinion is that the government should stay out of at least one part of our lives.

First of all, most people who run these small businesses are law-abiding citizens. Many of them have other jobs where they pay more than their share of taxes (unlike the wealthy, who pay almost none). Others are people who want jobs where they have to pay taxes, but can't find them.

Secondly, the government requires too much paperwork from small businesses. If these small businesspeople have to keep the complicated records that the tax people require, they won't have time to sell old furniture, prepare food for parties, or whatever their business involves.

Finally, and most importantly, the United States is supposed to be a free country, but the government interferes everywhere. Let us Americans be free at least in our own homes!

Al Melinowski
Union City, New Jersey

B. Answer these questions about the letter.

1. How does the letter begin and end?
2. How many paragraphs does the letter have? Are the paragraphs long or short? (Note that paragraphs in newspapers are often shorter than paragraphs in academic writing.)
3. What transition expressions does the writer use?
4. How does the writer support his opinions?

C. Write an opening sentence for your letter similar to the opening sentence of "Home Free." You can either write a response to "Luck or Thievery" or choose another article to respond to. Tell what article you are responding to and give your opinion.

_____

_____

PART TWO

DEVELOPING WRITING SKILLS

Developing Cohesion and Style

Stating Obligations and Opinions with Modals: *Must, Have to, Should, Ought to*

> You can show the strength of your opinion by the choice of the modal you use.

A. Which of the modals *must, have to, should,* and *ought to* show strong obligation or duty? Which show weaker obligation? Find an example of *should* and an example of *have to* in the letter to the editor on page 40. Why do you think the writer used those modals in those instances?

B. Make sentences using *must, must not, have to, not have to, should, should not,* or *ought to* about the following topics, depending on how strong you think the obligation is.

Example: Every working person *should* pay taxes, but many people don't.

1. paying taxes
2. drinking alcohol
3. drinking alcohol and then driving
4. spending a lot of money to clean up the environment
5. giving money to the poor
6. gambling
7. trying to find the owner of jewelry you found on the street
8. robbing a person's house if you need money
9. borrowing someone's car

Supporting an Opinion with a General Statement and Examples

A. Look at the second paragraph in the letter to the editor on page 40. It gives a general truth and then supports it with examples. What is the general truth? What are the examples?

_____

_____

_____

B. These sentences state general truths. Give one or two examples to support them.

1. The government loses millions of dollars every year because of people who don't pay their share of taxes.

_____

_____

2. Almost everyone gambles in one way or another.

_____

_____

3. Money is the root of all evil.

_____

_____

4. Lack of money is the root of much of the evil of our society.

_____

_____

5. When you find something on the street that someone has lost, it is almost impossible to find the owner.

_____

_____

C. Look at the reasons you gave for your opinion on the news report on page 38. Can you support any of them with examples?

Supporting an Opinion with Predictions

A. Look at the third paragraph in the letter to the editor. It supports a general statement with a prediction. What is the prediction?

_____

What verb tense is used in the *if* clause?

_____

What verb tense is used in the main clause?

_____

B. As a class or in groups, make predictions. What will happen if . . .

1. the government opens (or closes) gambling casinos in your city?
2. the government starts (or prohibits) a lottery in your city?
3. the government makes the wealthy pay more taxes?
4. the government cuts welfare payments?
5. everyone gives one-tenth of his or her income to charity?
6. fewer drunk drivers are on the road?
7. the government makes drinking alcohol illegal?
8. someone tries to return a valuable item he or she found on the street?

C. Look at the reasons you gave for your opinion on the news report. Can you support any of them with predictions?

Stating Opinions: Strong and Moderate

Some letters to the editor express opinions strongly and others moderately. A strong opinion does not allow for different points of view, whereas a moderate opinion does. When writers express their opinions strongly, they often involve their readers' emotions. When writers express their opinions moderately, they often use logical arguments.

A. Read the following expressions. Which of them are strong? Which are more moderate?

		STRONG	MODERATE
1.	I disagree with . . .	_____	_____
2.	. . . is hogwash!	_____	_____
3.	My opinion is that . . .	_____	_____
4.	. . . is immoral.	_____	_____
5.	. . . is the only logical solution.	_____	_____
6.	Only a fool would disagree with . . .	_____	_____
7.	I believe . . .	_____	_____
8.	In my opinion . . .	_____	_____
9.	. . . is absurd!	_____	_____

B. Create some sentences about the news report using the preceding expressions. Which do you think are more appropriate for your letter?

_____

_____

_____

_____

Writing the First Draft

Write your letter using the opening sentence you wrote. Give your opinions and the reasons for your opinions, supporting them with examples or predictions. Don't worry about grammar at this time. Write on every other line so you can revise your paragraph. Add transitions to your paragraph.

PART THREE

REVISING AND EDITING

Revising Your Writing

Avoiding Faulty Reasoning

When you revise a piece of writing that gives reasons for opinions, you should make sure that you haven't used *faulty reasoning*. Following are definitions and examples of different kinds of faulty reasoning.

1. False analogy: comparing two things that are not similar

   Example: Some people have to gamble. They are just like thieves because they can hurt other people.

2. Generalization: saying that something is true for all when it is only true for some, or making a general statement based on only a few cases

   Examples: All Americans are rich.
   There is a wealthy man who comes into the restaurant where I am a waiter and never leaves a tip. Rich men are stingy.
   (Note in this example the generalization follows the description of one particular case.)

3. Irrelevant argument: giving an example or reason that does not relate to the opinion

    Example: I don't think the accountant was embezzling money from his company because he has a nice family and always goes to church.

An irrelevant argument might also suggest that because one thing follows another, it relates to it, when it really doesn't.

    Example: Borrowing money always causes problems. Two days after Mario borrowed money, his wife asked for a divorce.

4. Begging the question: giving a reason that only restates the opinion in different words

    Example: Gambling is wrong because it is immoral.

A. The following statements are responses to the newspaper article you read, "Luck or Thievery." Identify the kind of faulty reasoning each one shows.

1. Everyone should return the money because the money should go back to the government.
2. I heard about a woman who got some of the money and didn't return it. The next day she fell and broke her leg. She knew she did the wrong thing.
3. Insurance companies always cheat people.
4. Picking up the money that fell onto the road is similar to picking flowers that grow in the forest.

B. Look at the reasons and examples you wrote in your letter. Do any of them show faulty reasoning?

C. Revise the letter you wrote. Check for the following items when you revise.

1. Content

    a. Did you state your opinions clearly?
    b. Did you support your opinions with examples?
    c. Did you include predictions?
    d. Did you avoid faulty reasoning?

2. Organization

    a. Did you write an opening sentence that told what article you are responding to, and give your opinion?
    b. Did you write a concluding sentence?

3. Cohesion and style

    a.   Did you use transitions?
    b.   Did you state your opinions using appropriate modals?
    c.   Did you use either a moderate or a strong style?

Editing Practice

Correcting Spelling Errors

> Always edit your writing for spelling errors. This is a good time to review the spelling rules in the appendix. However, you can't always count on rules to help you with spelling. Often you have to use a dictionary to check words you are not sure you have spelled correctly.

Correct these words if they are incorrect or write *correct* if they are correct. Use your dictionary if you are not sure.

1.   succesful _____
2.   moralety _____
3.   evil _____
4.   honnestly _____
5.   truely _____

6.   estimatted _____
7.   defendant _____
8.   prosecutor _____
9.   goverment _____
10. taxs _____

Correcting Syllabification Errors

> If a word is too long to fit at the end of the line, divide it between syllables and put the second part of the word on the next line. Don't divide words that have one syllable. Put at least three letters on each line, and use a hyphen after the first part of the divided word. Look at these examples:
>
> *Wrong:* Don't divide wo-
> rds that have
> one syllable.
>
> *Correct:* Don't divide
> words
> that have one
> syllable.
>
> owing
> *Wrong:* He's always borr
> money.
>
> *Correct:* He's always
> borrow-
> ing money.

General Rules for Syllabification

1. Divide words after prefixes or before suffixes.

   con-struc-tion   em-bez-zle-ment   com-fort-a-ble

2. Divide words between two consonants.

   col-lege   ad-dic-tion   com-pul-sive

If you are not sure how to divide a word, write the whole word on the next line or check your dictionary.

A. If these words would not fit at the end of a line, how would you divide them? Draw a line between syllables. Check your dictionary if necessary.

1. expensive
2. accounting
3. irrelevant
4. organization
5. consumer
6. generous
7. argument
8. immoral

B. Edit this paragraph. Find seventeen spelling errors, four syllabification errors, and three run-on sentences.

A Problem with Priorities

Pacific College spends too much money on activitys that are not related to educattion. One of the bigest expenses is ath-letics, for example, it has to pay for coaches' saliries, e-quipment, and building stadiems. It also sponsors a free st-udent newspaper and many student activaties such as partys, plays, and conserts. Many staf members spend a lot of time o-rganizing and planing these activities, they have to be paid salaries for this work as well. These activatys are fine, but not when the college is decresing libery hours on the weeke-nds and increasing class size I like football games, partys, and conserts, but I beleive that my educattion is more important.

Editing Your Writing

Edit the letter you wrote. You can also give it to a partner to check. Use this checklist.

GRAMMAR

1. Simple verb forms with modals
2. Verb forms with predictions and *if* clauses
3. No run-on sentences

FORM

1. Paragraph form: indentation, margins, capitals at the beginning of sentences
2. Spelling
3. Syllabification

Writing the Second Draft

After you edit your letter, rewrite it neatly, using good handwriting and correct form. Sign your name and your city at the bottom.

PART FOUR

COMMUNICATING THROUGH WRITING

Sharing

Exchange letters with another student and write a response to his or her opinion. Do you agree with your classmate? Why or why not?

Using Feedback

Look at your teacher's comments. If you don't understand something, ask about it.

Look at the three assignments you have completed so far and at the feedback sheets for each of them. Complete this list.

WHAT I DO WELL WHEN I WRITE

_____

_____

_____

_____

_____

_____

_____

WHAT I NEED TO IMPROVE

_____

_____

_____

_____

_____

Developing Your Skills

A. Look at a local or school newspaper or a weekly news magazine and find the letters to the editor. Often some are logical and others are emotional; some are serious and others try to be funny. Which letters do you like? Do they give strong or moderate opinions?

B. Find an article that interests you in a newspaper and write a letter in response to it.

C. Make an editorial page for a class newsletter. Write editorials and letters to the editor.

D. Have you experienced or read about a strange happening like the one the newspaper article on page 38 describes? Write a description of the happening.

Developing Fluency

A. Write your reaction to one of the proverbs or sayings at the beginning of this chapter or one a classmate has told.

B. Ask a classmate if you can read a selection from his or her journal. Write your reaction to the selection.

4

JOBS AND PROFESSIONS

GETTING READY TO WRITE

Exploring Ideas

Discussing Accomplishments

Many colleges and employers ask questions about people's past experience. On the next page, look at the questions from various application forms. Then discuss the reactions of the students in the picture to the question "What have you accomplished in the last two years?" What do you think about their reactions?

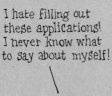

Tell us something about yourself that will help us know you better.

Write a short personal history.

How have you been able to contribute to your community?

Write about the most difficult thing you have ever done.

Discuss your duties in your previous or present job.

Building Vocabulary

A. Discuss the meanings of these personal characteristics. Add to the list other characteristics that people who are successful in school or work should have.

concerned about other people
_____
creative
disciplined
_____
enthusiastic
_____
hard-working
having a good sense of humor
_____
self-confident
_____
trustworthy
_____

B. In small groups, choose three of the people below and discuss how their experiences show that they have characteristics that are important to success in work and school.

1. Miguel's mother works afternoons, so he has taken care of his younger brother after school for the last four years.
2. Yoshi taught himself how to play the guitar and plays in a band.
3. Greta works as a salesclerk in her uncle's store.
4. Shenner has been studying English for the last nine months with money he got from a scholarship as the top student in his class.
5. Paulo likes to create computer games.
6. Ana is a bicyclist and takes long trips on her bicycle.
7. Sophia has been raising three children for the last eight years.
8. Josh drank a lot of alcohol in high school. He decided to quit drinking and hasn't had a drink in two years.
9. All of Parvin's friends tell her their problems.

C. Discuss one or two experiences you could write about on a job or college application form. How does the experience show you have qualities that are important for success?

D. On a separate page, describe the qualities of four of the people from Exercise B. Create examples that show that the people have these qualities.

Example: Miguel is disciplined and trustworthy. Often when he wanted to go out with his friends, he stayed home because he didn't want to leave his younger brother alone. His mother knew she could trust him.

E. Write notes about the qualities that best describe you. Describe experiences that show you have these qualities. Use a separate piece of paper.

Organizing Ideas

Limiting Information

A. Look at the beginning of the following first draft of a personal description. The writer hasn't limited what he wants to say. Is it easy to read? Cross out the information he should leave out.

> I have learned a lot working as a messenger in New York City. First of all, I have learned to persevere when there are difficulties. I also find math very difficult, but I have a tutor now who has been a great help to me. So many times I have wanted to quit, but I have tried to keep my sense of humor. I have had problems with drivers who almost run me over, constant rain for weeks at a time, unreadable addresses, and rude customers. I think the drivers in New York are the worst in any city I have seen. I have also learned that even the most routine job can be interesting.

B. In this chapter, you are going to write about one experience that shows your positive characteristics. Look at the notes you just made and choose the experience you are going to write about and the qualities it shows you have. Cross out the other experiences or qualities.

Writing Topic Sentences

> The topic sentence for your paragraph should make the reader interested in you. It should show how you're special and should be positive, focusing on your good points.
>
> These are topic sentences some students wrote for their paragraphs. Which ones do you like? Why?
>
> 1. I have always danced just for fun, but I recently realized that dancing has been an important learning experience for me.
> 2. I guess a lot of people take care of their children, so it isn't very special.
> 3. Two years ago, my family and I immigrated to Vancouver, Canada, and my life changed.
> 4. A very important thing has been happening.

5. Although I was born in Vietnam, I have been living in a small town in Texas for the last three years, and the two cultures have affected me in many important ways.
6. My relationship with my children has developed my creativity, discipline, and sense of humor.
7. Last year I had a very bad experience.
8. I like to go dancing a lot.

Writing Concluding Sentences

The kind of paragraph you will write needs a concluding sentence. It can tell what you learned about yourself from the experience you chose, or it can describe a hope for the future. It should leave the reader with a positive feeling.
These are examples of good concluding sentences. Why are they good?

1. I hope that my experience raising my own children will help me be a better teacher.
2. I feel that I've experienced the best of both cultures, and I hope to use this experience in my future work.
3. Now I know that if I enjoy something and know it is important, I can work really hard to make it a success.

These are examples of poor concluding sentences. Why are they poor?

1. I never want to go through such a horrible experience again.
2. I guess raising children isn't easy for anyone.
3. I can never do things I don't enjoy, but when I like something I work pretty hard at it.

In a small group, tell the other students what experience you are going to write about. Discuss some possible concluding sentences you can use.

PART TWO

DEVELOPING WRITING SKILLS

Developing Cohesion and Style

Using the Correct Tense: Past Versus Present Perfect

Key to Choosing Past or Present Perfect

PAST TENSE

Completion of action, state, time, or relevance of event

Example: I came to Boston in 1986. (Before that, I lived in Houston.)

PRESENT PERFECT TENSE

Incompletion of action, state, time, or relevance of event

Example: Every year since 1986 I have come to Boston for Christmas vacation. (I still come to Boston every year.)

Choose the correct tense of the verb, past or present perfect, for these sentences. To choose, ask yourself the question, "Is the action, state, time, or relevance of the event completed or not?"

Examples: (You live in Detroit.) I *have lived* (live) in Detroit for three years.

(You live in Seattle.) I _*lived*_ (live) in Detroit for three years.

1. (You're fifty years old.) I _____ (raise) two children.

2. (You're thirty years old and expect to have more children.) I _____ (raise) two children.

3. I _____ (have) two jobs this year.

4. I _____ (have) two jobs last year.

5. (You have immigrated.) I _____ (learn) a lot when I was waiting to immigrate.

6. I _____ (learn) a lot in my life.

7. I _____ (work) in this store for a month now.

8. I _____ (work) in a store for a month, but then I quit.

Using the Correct Tense: Present Perfect Versus Present Perfect Continuous

---

Key to Choosing Present Perfect or Present Perfect Continuous

PRESENT PERFECT

Nonaction verbs: *be, have* (for possession), *like, know, mean,* etc.

Example: They have known about this since last month (for a long time).

Other verbs: *study, work, live, experience, think, help, make,* etc. These verbs express noncontinuous or nonrepeated actions.

Example: I haven't gone there lately. I have gone there twice.

PRESENT PERFECT CONTINUOUS

This tense expresses continuous or repeated actions.

Example: I have been swimming a lot lately.

Sometimes either the present perfect or the present perfect continuous can be correct, but the present perfect continuous stresses the continuous or repeated nature of the event.

Examples: They've been to that restaurant.

They've been going to that restaurant (once a week for months).

A. Choose the correct tense, present perfect or present perfect continuous. First ask if the verb is nonaction. If it is another verb (not a nonaction verb), ask if the sentence stresses continuous or ongoing action.

  Examples: I *have known* (know) about this for a long time.

  I *have been thinking* (think) about this since yesterday.

  1. He _____ (work) with me since 1988—we still work together at the same place.

  2. Has he ever _____ (work) in a restaurant?

  3. I _____ (not write) my essay yet.

  4. I usually write every day, but I _____ (not write) much lately.

  5. She _____ already _____ (fill out) her application.

  6. She _____ (fill out) her application for the last four hours.

B. Complete these paragraphs with the simple past, present perfect, or present perfect continuous forms of the verbs in parentheses.

     I _____ (like) to write since I _____ (be) five years old.
                1   2
When I first _____ (hold) a pen in my hand and carefully
                          3
_____ (draw) the beautiful Japanese characters, I
    4
_____ (know) I _____ (want) to be a writer. Ever
    5   6
since that day I _____ (write) in my free time. When I
                      7
_____ (come) to Miami six months ago to study English, I
    8
_____ (not realize) that I would feel so frustrated. I _____
    9   10
(have) the thoughts of a nineteen-year-old but the skills of a three-year-old!

     Although I _____ (study) hard since that day, I still
                           11
_____ (not write) an essay in English that I can be proud of.
    12
This experience _____ (be) frustrating, but I _____
                      13   14
(learn) a lot from it. For six months I _____ (experience)
                                         15
the world through the words of another culture. I _____ (learn) dif-
                                                       16
ferent ways of communicating and can use these new methods in my
writing in Japanese.

Using Demonstratives to Unify a Paragraph

> A good writer uses phrases with *this, that, these,* or *those*—demonstratives—to
> refer to ideas in previous sentences.

A. Underline the phrases with demonstratives in Exercise B above. What words or
ideas do they refer to?

B. Complete these sentences with *this, that, these,* or *those.* Use *this* or *these* to refer to ideas or events in the present or recent past. Use *that* or *those* to refer to ideas or events farther in the past.

1. I first began to play soccer when I was four years old, and I have spent some of my happiest moments since _____ time on the soccer field.

2. A very important holiday in China is New Year's. On _____ day, we have a big feast.

3. My favorite aunt died recently. _____ experience was sad and frightening because no one close to me had ever died before. However, it has made me see life differently.

4. I have learned French, Hungarian, and Spanish, and I'm now learning English. I love the different qualities of each of _____ languages.

C. Prepositional phrases with demonstratives often appear at the beginning of sentences to unify a paragraph. Add one of the following phrases to the second sentence in each of the numbered items. Use a demonstrative in each phrase.

for _____ reason	on _____ day	in _____ city
in _____ school	because of _____ factors	during _____ years

1. Two years and six months ago, my first child was born. My life changed.

   _____

   _____

2. I lived in Thailand from the age of seven to eleven. My parents' only hope was going to live in America.

   _____

   _____

3. I have always been shy. Learning a new language is a challenge for me.

   _____

   _____

4. I came to Miami two years ago. I have had many new experiences.

    _____

    _____

5. However, I was too short and was not thin enough. I could not continue to dance professionally.

    _____

    _____

6. I came to the International English Program six months ago. I have made many new friends.

    _____

    _____

Writing the First Draft

Write your paragraph. You can use the ideas you wrote in the beginning of the chapter if you wish, as well as your topic sentence and concluding sentence. You can also use the demonstratives *this, that, these,* and *those* to unify your paragraph. Write on every other line so you can revise your paragraph easily.

PART THREE

REVISING AND EDITING

Revising Your Writing

Omitting Unimportant Ideas

A. Read this paragraph. The writer has a lot of good ideas, but some of the ideas aren't important or don't give new information. What ideas should she omit? Can she combine ideas to make the paragraph shorter?

> I have been taking an English class for the last six months. This has meant a rewarding but difficult change in my life. Before that I spent all my time raising my family, a daughter who is now five and a son who is three. My daughter's name is Karen. She is in kindergarten and my son now goes to day-care. Because I did not speak much English, my focus was my home and my neighborhood, where I felt comfortable and could speak Spanish. I spoke only Spanish at home and in my neighborhood. When I

needed to take my children to the doctor or speak with my landlord, my younger sisters translated for me. One of them would go with me and speak to the doctor in English and then tell me what he said in Spanish. Now I have become more independent. I have learned a lot from my classmates and I have also realized that as a mother I have had many experiences that they are interested in. Now my sisters tell me to speak to the doctor or landlord myself. I go to stores where I have to speak English and I speak English in the clinic where I take my son to the doctor. This was very difficult at first, but I have been feeling more and more comfortable about my ability to communicate with other English speakers. I hope to use this new confidence to get a job.

B. Revise the paragraph you wrote. Answer these questions about it.

1. Content

   a. Does your paragraph describe your best characteristics?
   b. Does it show that you will be successful in what you want to do?

2. Organization

   a. Do you have too many or too few ideas for one paragraph? Talk to a partner about how you can limit your topic or add more ideas.
   b. Are all your ideas about one topic? Cross out ideas that are not important or are not about the topic.
   c. Is your topic sentence positive? Does it make you sound special and interesting?
   d. Does each sentence add a new idea? Your sentences shouldn't just repeat the same idea in different words. Rewrite the repetitive sentences or take them out.
   e. Does your concluding sentence tell something you've learned about yourself or something you hope for in the future?

3. Cohesion and style

    a. Have you used verb tenses correctly?
    b. Can you add demonstratives (*this, that, these, those*) to unify your paragraph?

C. Revise your first draft.

Editing Practice

Using Correct Capitalization; Using Correct Verb Forms

A. Review the rules for capitalization in the appendix at the back of the book and correct the capitalization in these sentences if necessary.

1. Because my Mother doesn't speak english, I have to translate for her.

2. When I first moved to the southwest, I got a job as a Salesman.

3. I have lived in miami, Los Angeles, and dallas.

4. I received a Scholarship from Grant college in the Spring and started classes in september.

5. This semester I am taking Math, physics, english, and Government.

B. Some of the underlined words and phrases in the following paragraph are correct, and some contain errors. Correct the mistakes.

I <u>have been worked</u> since I <u>have had</u> nine years old, and I like to work. When I <u>was having</u> nine, we <u>was</u> in El <u>s</u>alvador and we <u>was</u> very poor. I <u>pick</u> coffee with my mother and brothers. It was hard work to carry the heavy coffee bags, which <u>had weighed</u> as much as one hundred pounds, up and down hills. But I learned to work with other people. For the last two years I <u>been working</u> as a gardener in the <u>u</u>nited <u>s</u>tates. Many people want me to come and work in their gardens, and I <u>have learn</u> a lot about <u>amer</u>-icans. I <u>have even learn</u> to speak some <u>E</u>nglish. I like my job because it's different every day, and I can be outdoors.

Editing Your Writing

Edit the paragraph you wrote. You can also give it to a partner to check. Use this checklist.

GRAMMAR

1. Verb tenses
2. No run-on sentences
3. Use of demonstratives

FORM

1. Paragraph form: margins, indentation
2. Capitalization
3. Spelling and syllabification

Writing the Second Draft

After you edit your paragraph, rewrite it neatly, using good handwriting and correct form.

PART FOUR

COMMUNICATING THROUGH WRITING

Give your paragraph to your teacher for comments.

Sharing

In small groups, share your paragraphs with one another. Talk about what positive characteristics the paragraphs show and give the reasons why the paragraphs would impress an employer or college.

Using Feedback

Look at your teacher's comments. If you don't understand something, ask about it. Answer these questions about your writing.

1. Has your writing changed since you began this class? How has it changed?
2. What have you learned from this course?
3. How do you feel about the way you write?
4. What do you like about writing?
5. What is most difficult for you about writing?
6. What can you do to improve your writing?

Developing Your Skills

A. Look in your school or city library for instructions on how to complete job and college applications. Following the instructions, fill out a sample application and have your classmates or teacher check it. Pay special attention to spelling, neat handwriting, and capitalization. Follow all directions carefully.

B. Some applications ask for an autobiography or a personal history. Expand the paragraph you wrote for this section into an autobiography. Don't just list events in your life. Explain why they were important and what you learned from them. Finish the autobiography with a paragraph describing your future goals.

Developing Fluency

A. Write as much as you can in ten minutes about a person you respect. Write about the characteristics or experiences of that person that make you respect him or her.

B. Write about a job you'd love to have or the job you'd hate the most.

C. Write about whatever comes to mind.

5

LIFESTYLES

GETTING READY TO WRITE

Exploring Ideas

Discussing Lessons People Learn from Experience

A. Read the following list of "lessons"—things that people learn from experience. In a small group, discuss the lessons. Do you agree with all of the lessons? Try to think of experiences that might teach someone each of the lessons.

It's important to me to think for myself.

Self-discipline is an essential quality.

Sometimes you have to take risks in order to win.

Friendship is one of the most valuable things in life.

You should never make promises you can't keep.

If you want a good marriage, you have to compromise.

Change can bring excitement.

Sometimes parents really do know best.

Sometimes it's best to lie to the people you love.

Hard work can be satisfying.

Independence is enjoyable.

B. In the same group, study the four pictures above. Choose a lesson from the preceding list to fit each picture.

C. Make up a story for one of the pictures to show how the experience taught a lesson.

D. Think of an experience that taught you a lesson and write about it. The lesson might be one from the list or it might be another lesson. Write the lesson in a sentence at the top of a piece of paper and draw a line under it. Then write for ten minutes about the experience that taught you that lesson. Don't worry about correctness or organization now.

Building Vocabulary

A. Add to this list the new words you learned in your discussion or the words you used in your writing.

Nouns		Verbs	Adjectives
decision	_____	compromise	essential
excitement		lie	valuable
friendship	_____	take risks	
importance	_____		_____
independence		_____	_____
marriage	_____		
promise	_____	_____	_____
self-discipline			
	_____	_____	_____
	_____		
	_____	_____	_____

B. Is it possible to use any of the words in the list—or different forms of the words—as different parts of speech? Make a list of the parts of speech on a separate page. Check your dictionary if necessary.

Example: Noun   Verb   Adjective

              importance   —   important

C. Using some of the adjectives from your list, create sentences with prepositional phrases.

Example: Friendship is very *important to me.*

Organizing Ideas

Understanding Anecdotes

An anecdote is a short description of something that really happened. Writers use anecdotes to illustrate or explain ideas. In this chapter, you will write an anecdote about something that happened to you and that taught you a lesson about life.

Many anecdotes or stories do not have topic sentences because stories are usually easy to understand. Your anecdote should answer these questions:

1. *When* and *where* did the story take place?
2. *Who* was involved and *what* was their relationship?
3. *What* happened?
4. *Why* did it happen?
5. *What* was the result?

A. Read the anecdote that follows and discuss it with your classmates. Does it answer all the preceding questions? Which questions does most of the story answer? Which questions does it answer in the first two sentences? Which does it answer in the last sentence?

One summer weekend some friends and I decided to walk to a water-fall we had heard about. Since it was too far to walk along the road, we followed a railroad line. We had walked five or six miles when we came to a high rock wall where the tracks entered a tunnel. This tunnel didn't look very long, but it was narrow and we knew it would be dangerous if a train came. However, we couldn't climb the rocks or walk around them and no one wanted to go back. Finally we decided to go through. I knew it was foolish, but I went because the others did.

As soon as we entered the tunnel, we saw that it was longer and darker than we had thought. Suddenly everyone was frightened and we all began to run. "This is crazy!" I thought. "Why didn't I go back?" We ran faster and it got lighter in the tunnel. Then we were outside and we fell on the ground gasping. About a minute later a train came through. That was when I finally realized the importance of thinking for myself.

When writing an anecdote, you might begin a new paragraph for several different reasons. Here are some of them:

1. The time or place of the story changes.

2. You begin to tell about a new person.

3. Something important happens in the story.

4. You stop telling the story and explain something about it.

B. In the anecdote about the tunnel, what was the writer's reason for starting a new paragraph when he wrote "As soon as we entered the tunnel . . ."?

Using Details

Your anecdote will be more interesting if you can make the reader "live" the experience with you. One way to do this is by using details to help the reader see what you saw and feel what you felt. Here is the second paragraph of the tunnel anecdote without the details that make it seem more real. What details did the writer leave out?

> We started to walk through the tunnel, but then we got frightened and started to run. After we got outside a train came through. That was when I finally realized the importance of thinking for myself.

One difficulty with details is that they can easily become *digressions:*

> One summer weekend some friends and I decided to walk to a waterfall we had heard about. This waterfall was called Horsetail Falls because it looked like a horse's tail. There was a place to swim at the bottom and it was a wonderful place for a picnic ...

In a good anecdote, everything leads to the conclusion. If a detail leads away from the lesson (even if it is true and interesting), take it out of your anecdote.

Here are the writer's notes for part of the tunnel anecdote. Discuss the questions that follow.

> didn't look very long
> narrow, dangerous
> rocks 80–100 ft. high—couldn't climb them
> river on left
> sharp brambles, more rocks on right
> couldn't go right or left
> no trains all day—maybe tracks not used?

1. Which details did the writer leave out of the anecdote?
2. Do you agree with his decisions?

PART TWO

DEVELOPING WRITING SKILLS

Developing Cohesion and Style

Using the Past Perfect Tense

> In the anecdote about the tunnel, everything happened in the past. The writer used mainly past-tense verbs to tell the story in the order that it happened. But three times the writer looked back in time and used the past perfect tense to write about what *had happened earlier.*

A. Find the three sentences in the anecdote that used the past perfect tense. What event happened earlier in each sentence? What happened later? Complete the following chart.

In the Anecdote	Happened Earlier	Happened Later
1. We _____ to walk to a waterfall we _____ about.		
2. We _____ five or six miles when we _____ to a high rock wall.		
3. We _____ that it was longer and darker than we _____.		

B. The following passage is an early draft of the tunnel anecdote. (You will notice that it still has a lot of digressions.) Fill in the blanks with the past tense or the past perfect tense of the verbs in parentheses.

One summer weekend some friends and I decided to take a picnic to a waterfall we had heard about. Some people _____ (drive) cars and
_____ (take) the food, but the rest of us _____ (want) to
walk. Since it was too far to walk along the road, we followed a railroad line. We had walked five or six miles when we came to a high rock wall where the tracks entered a tunnel. We _____ (be) surprised. Nobody
_____ (tell) us about it. The tunnel didn't look very long, but it was
narrow and we knew it would be dangerous if a train came. However, we couldn't climb the rocks or go around them, and no one wanted to go back. I _____ (have) a good breakfast, but some of the others
_____ (not eat). They _____ (want) to get to the waterfall
and have lunch. Finally we decided to go through. I knew it was foolish, but I went because the others did.

As soon as we entered the tunnel, we saw that it was longer and darker than we had thought. Earlier we _____ (decide) to walk and to stay
together, but suddenly everyone was frightened and we all began to run. "This is crazy," I thought. "Why didn't I go back?" We ran faster and it got lighter in the tunnel. Then we were outside and we fell on the ground gasping. No one _____ (fall) in the tunnel. We _____ (be)
all safe. About a minute later a train came through.

We _____ (be) upset because we _____ (come) so close
to death. We _____ also angry with ourselves for being so foolish.
Later we _____ (hear) that two boys _____ (die) in that
tunnel the month before. That was when I finally realized the importance of thinking for myself.

Writing the First Draft

Now you are ready to write your own anecdote. Use the experience you wrote about earlier or choose another experience. Be sure to choose one that taught you a clear lesson. Write on every other line so you can revise your paragraph easily.

PART THREE

REVISING AND EDITING

Revising Your Writing

Omitting Digressions and Unimportant Details

A. The following paragraph is the first part of an anecdote. The last sentence of the anecdote will be, "That was when I learned the satisfaction of doing hard work well." Revise the paragraph by taking out digressions and details that do not lead to the lesson of the anecdote. Use one line to cross them out. (You don't have to fix the grammar after you do this.)

The year I was fifteen my parents sent me to work on my uncle's farm for the summer. It was in South Carolina and they had peach trees, and cows and chickens. They didn't make much money and my father was always telling my uncle to sell the farm and come to Chicago. I didn't want to go and I didn't like it when I got there. It was very hot and muggy most of the time. My cousins got up at 4:30 in the morning and went to bed at 9:00 at night and in between they worked. I had never worked on a farm

before, and my cousin Wayne had to teach me everything, like milking the cows, driving the tractor, and so on. We were the same age, but I was bigger than he was. I was already six feet tall. Even so I couldn't do anything as well as he could. I had a lot of friends at home and we always hung around together, especially in summer. I used to think about them. "They don't have to work on some dumb farm," I thought. "How come I have to?"

B. Compare your revision to your classmates' work. Did you take out the same things? Discuss your choices.

C. Answer these questions about the anecdote you wrote and then revise it.

    1. Content

        a. Have you told an interesting story?
        b. Does the lesson (conclusion) fit the story you told?
        c. Have you given enough information so that your anecdote is easy to understand?
        d. Have you used details to make the story more interesting and real?

    2. Organization

        a. Have you avoided unimportant details and digressions?
        b. Have you used paragraph divisions to make the story clearer or more interesting?

    3. Cohesion and style

    Have you used transition words and varied your sentence patterns?

Editing Practice

Punctuating Direct Speech

JOE: Hello.	"Hello," said Joe. Joe said, "Hello."
JUDY: Wait!	"Wait!" shouted Judy. "Wait!" she shouted.
MR. KIM: Are you ready? Let's go.	"Are you ready?" asked Mr. Kim. "Let's go." "Are you ready?" he asked. "Let's go."

A. Put these words in the right order and punctuate the sentences. Check your work with two or three classmates.

1. time she asked it is what _____

_____

2. hello Mrs. Brown how you are said _____

_____

3. I is crazy this thought _____

_____

B. The following paragraph is the second part of the anecdote at the beginning of Part Three. In this paragraph, check punctuation and word order in the direct speech and make corrections if necessary. Also, correct the underlined verbs if they are wrong.

I'm there about two weeks when Wayne and I have to load some bales of hay. After half an hour we loaded a lot of bales and it was getting hard to throw them up onto the wagon. "I'm going to miss the next one I thought." But Wayne missed first. His bale didn't go high enough and it has fallen back down. I took a deep breath and throw mine. I did it! Hey Dad Wayne called. "Did you see that?" I did it again and they cheer. I felt wonderful. After that everything change. Wayne and I were friends and we enjoy competing with each other in everything. Usually he was better, but sometimes I am. I worked hard all summer and I love it. I learn a lot that summer, but the most important lesson is that day in the hayfield. That was when I learn the satisfaction of doing hard work well.

Editing Your Writing

Edit the anecdote you wrote. You can also give it to a partner to check. Use this checklist.

GRAMMAR

Past, present perfect, and past perfect tenses

FORM

1. Punctuation of direct speech
2. Spelling and capitalization

Writing the Second Draft

After you edit your anecdote, rewrite it neatly, using good handwriting and correct form.

PART FOUR

COMMUNICATING THROUGH WRITING

Sharing

Read the anecdotes of two of your classmates. Then answer these questions about each anecdote.

1. What exactly made the anecdote interesting for you? Be specific. You can mention the incidents, some of the details, the lesson, or something else.
2. Do you agree with the student's conclusion (lesson) or not? Briefly explain why or why not.

Give your anecdote to your teacher for comments.

Using Feedback

Look at your teacher's comments. If you don't understand something, ask about it. Discuss these questions with some of your classmates.

1. What was easy about the writing in this chapter?
2. What was hard?
3. Why do you think writers like to use anecdotes in their writing?

Developing Your Skills

A. Columnists who write for newspapers often include anecdotes in their columns. These columns often appear on the front, back, or editorial pages. Check your local paper and try to find a column with an anecdote. Read it and tell the anecdote to the rest of your small group or class. Was there a lesson to the anecdote? What was the point of the anecdote?

B. Many people have anecdotes they tell over and over because the anecdote is interesting or funny. Think of an anecdote that you or a friend or relative likes to tell. Write the anecdote.

Developing Fluency

A. Write about a frustrating day or experience you've had recently.

B. Write about the thing that makes you most angry.

C. Write about the thing that makes you most happy.

6

TRAVEL AND TRANSPORTATION

GETTING READY TO WRITE

Exploring Ideas

Discussing Long-distance Transportation

> There are various ways to travel from one city to another. Besides going by car, the most common ways to travel are by bus, train, or plane.

A. Look at the following list of advantages and disadvantages of travel by train. Can you add advantages or disadvantages to the list?

An airline attendant serving a meal to passengers in an airplane

Train Travel

Advantages

fairly safe

trains have dining cars so you don't have to stop to eat

trains have sleeping cars or seats so you don't have to stay in hotels

usually cheaper than automobile travel for one person

gives you the chance to meet people and see the countryside

most trains have air conditioning, which a car might not have

_____

_____

Disadvantages

for several people, more expensive than by car

not as fast as by plane

may have to sit near people who talk a lot

may not be able to smoke

can't stop where you like

_____

_____

_____

B. Make a list of advantages and disadvantages of travel by plane.

Airplane Travel

Advantages	Disadvantages
_____	_____
_____	_____
_____	_____
_____	_____
_____	_____
_____	_____
_____	_____

Building Vocabulary

> The advantages and disadvantages of different forms of transportation can fit into certain categories.

Write words from your discussion in the following lists.

Speed	Comfort or Lack of Comfort	Convenience or Inconvenience
supersonic	*crowded*	*airport shuttle*
_____	*cramped*	_____
_____	_____	_____
_____	_____	_____

Safety	Economy or Expense
air traffic control	*expensive*
_____	*supersaver fare*
_____	_____
_____	_____

Organizing Ideas

Using Outside Sources of Information

Your composition will be about the advantages and disadvantages of public transportation within a city. You will get information for it from a transcript of an interview.

Here is a transcript of another interview about ten-speed racing bicycles. A magazine writer named Paul Fritz is interviewing Neil Pozos, the owner of a bicycle shop and president of the Hard Riders Cycling Club. Read the transcript and discuss it with your classmates. What advantages of ten-speed racing bicycles do they mention? What disadvantages do they mention? What other information can you find in the transcript? What purpose does the other information have? (*Hint:* Look for information that gives *background* for the subject.)

FRITZ: How many members do you have in the Hard Riders?

POZOS: Almost 2,000, and this is only our fourth year.

FRITZ: That's impressive. Cycling wasn't always so popular, was it?

POZOS: No. It really took off during the '70s. That was when physical fitness got fashionable and cycling expanded along with all the other sports.

FRITZ: Why do people take up cycling instead of jogging, for example, or tennis?

POZOS: Well, it's great exercise, it's more fun than jogging, it doesn't require great coordination . . .

FRITZ: Do most of your members ride ten-speed racing bikes?

POZOS: Yes, almost all of them. That's another trend that started in the '70s. Before then most of the bikes sold in this country were for kids. When adults rode bikes, they were usually three-speed touring bikes. Now most adults choose racers.

FRITZ: Why is that?

POZOS: Because they're lightweight and built for speed. Also, most of our members ride fifty, a hundred, two hundred miles a week. The racers let them go fast on level ground and slower going up hills with the same amount of work. It's a steady pace.

FRITZ: So they don't get so tired.

POZOS: Right.

FRITZ: Aren't racing bikes pretty delicate, though, when you compare them to other kinds?

POZOS: Yes, they are. They need frequent maintenance and adjustment and it's easy to damage them on rough roads, for example. They're uncomfortable on rough roads too. They're really not designed for that.

FRITZ: Are repairs expensive?

POZOS: Compared to other bikes, yes.

FRITZ: And racers cost a lot too, don't they?

POZOS: Sure. They're expensive to manufacture, so they have to cost more.

FRITZ: I get the feeling that a lot of people buy racing bikes just for the prestige—they don't really need such good bikes.

POZOS: That's true. It's a status thing with a lot of people—like driving an expensive car. I'd say that unless you want to race or you ride more than twenty or thirty miles a week you should get a cheaper bicycle—maybe a three-speed.

Listing Information

A. Use the interview transcript to complete these lists of the advantages and disadvantages of ten-speed racing bicycles. The lists are notes that Paul Fritz might have made in preparation for writing his article. For that reason, the lists use single words and short phrases, not sentences. This makes it easier to choose the best sentence structures while writing the first draft.

Ten-speed Racing Bicycles

Advantages   Disadvantages

light and fast   *delicate — easy to damage*

_____   _____

_____   _____

_____   _____

B. In the same way, list the background information you found in the transcript.

_____

_____

_____

_____

_____

Analyzing the Organization of a Composition

This is the article that Paul Fritz wrote after his interview with Neil Pozos.

The physical fitness craze that began in the 1970s is still big business today. Among the many groups that are making money from it are bicycle manufacturers, importers, and dealers. Although all kinds of bicycles are selling well today, the greatest increase has occurred in ten-speed racing bicycles.

These lightweight bicycles offer several advantages. They are usually well made and of high-quality materials. The rider can choose a gear for maximum speed on level ground or for minimum effort in climbing a hill. They allow the rider to work at a steady rate, so that he or she becomes less tired during a long ride. In addition, a ten-speed racer shows that its owner is serious about cycling.

© RUSSELL DIXON LAMB/PHOTO RESEARCHERS

On the other hand, racing bicycles also have some disadvantages. For one thing, they are expensive to buy and to maintain. They are more delicate than other bicycles, and as a result they need repair more often. Furthermore, they are extremely uncomfortable to ride on rough roads.

All in all, racing bicycles are not ideal for every cyclist. People who want a bicycle for running errands or spending Sundays in the park should buy a cheaper, simpler bicycle. However, serious fitness buffs and cyclists who are interested in speed will be happiest with a ten-speed racer.

In small groups, answer these questions about the article.

1. What is the main idea of each paragraph? Are the main ideas in the topic sentences of the paragraphs?
2. Does the article use all the information you wrote in your lists?
3. Does the article contain any facts or examples that were not in the interview?
4. What are some of the transition words and expressions the author uses?
5. Does the introduction give enough background information on the topic? Does the conclusion leave you with a positive feeling?

Choosing a Title

Like a topic sentence, a title should express the main idea of a composition and catch the readers' attention. In academic writing, titles are usually informative; in magazine writing (like Paul Fritz's article), they are usually "catchy," or interesting. Titles are almost always single words or phrases rather than sentences.

Which is the best title for Paul Fritz's article? Why? Discuss your choice with your classmates.

1. Why You Should Choose a Ten-speed Racing Bicycle
2. Cycling Becomes More Popular
3. Ten-speed Bicycles Have Advantages and Disadvantages
4. Advantages and Disadvantages of Ten-speed Bicycles
5. The Ten-speed Option
6. The Ten-speed Revolution
7. How Ten-speed Bicycles Work

PART TWO

DEVELOPING WRITING SKILLS

Developing Cohesion and Style

Choosing the Right Part of Speech

> In Part One you listed some terms relating to advantages and disadvantages of travel by airplane. In your writing for this chapter, you may need to use other forms of these words.

A. Complete the following chart with the correct parts of speech (nouns, verbs, adjectives, or *-ly* adverbs) corresponding to the word in the list. Use your dictionary if you wish. Your teacher may ask you to add other words from the class discussion.

Noun	Verb	Adjective	*-ly* Adverb
economy	to economize	economical	economically
convenience	—	_____	_____
comfort	_____	_____	_____
_____	_____	crowded	—
_____	spend	expensive	_____
safety	_____	_____	_____
air conditioning	_____	_____	—

B. Complete each sentence with the correct part of speech of the word in parentheses. If you need to add a verb, be sure to use the right tense and form.

1. The most important thing to me about the way I travel is that I choose a method that is not too _____ (expense).

2. My grandparents live in Florida and they want to be _____ (comfort) so they got a car with _____ (air-conditioned).

3. Airports have traffic control people to make sure the planes take off and land _____ (safe).

4. If you want to _____ (economy) on plane travel, try to buy your ticket in advance.

5. The problem with subways and buses is that sometimes there are

_____ (crowded) of people on them and it's hard to find a

seat.

6. A very _____ (convenience) way to travel is by automobile.

Writing the First Draft

A. Read the following transcript of an interview between a student, Tim, and a bus rider, Ann. Take notes on it. List the advantages and disadvantages of public transportation.

TIM: Why have you decided to use public transportation to get to work?

ANN: Well, the main reason is to save money. I might be able to afford a used car right now, but the expense of operating it—gas, repairs, and insurance—would be too much for me.

TIM: Well, that makes sense. But isn't public transportation rather inconvenient in this city? With a car, you can go where you want, when you want.

ANN: Right. And this is a real car town, so the bus system isn't as efficient as it could be. You have to wait a long time for the bus, and you often have to transfer at least one time to get where you're going.

TIM: And there aren't any other options as far as public transportation goes, are there?

ANN: No, there are no plans to build a subway system at this time.

TIM: What are some other benefits of using public transportation?

ANN: Well, it causes less pollution of the environment. Even though buses do contribute to air pollution, one bus carrying thirty people does much less harm than thirty people all driving their individual cars. Also, if you take a bus you don't have to worry about traffic or about finding parking, both of which are problems in this city.

TIM: Now, do you feel that, as a woman, you're safe taking the bus home late at night?

ANN: It certainly would be safer to be driving in your own car late at night, but the bus stops are well lit, and I'm usually going to and from highly populated areas at night. But there are definitely parts of town where I would not wait for or ride the bus late at night.

TIM: Well, it sounds as though you've made the right choice for yourself.

ANN: I certainly plan to get a car someday, as soon as I'm making enough money to maintain one. With a car you can take friends places and carry large loads, which could really come in handy.

B. Discuss the notes you made with a partner. You may want to add other ideas from the discussion to your list.

C. You can write your title either before or after you write the first draft. If you write it first, it might help you focus on the topic. If you write it afterward, you can make it fit the draft you wrote. You may want to write the title before the first draft and then revise it if necessary at the same time you revise the draft.

D. Write the first draft of your article about the advantages and disadvantages of public transportation within a city. You can use the same basic organization in your article as in the one on racing bicycles. However, you may organize your article differently, if you want.

PART THREE

REVISING AND EDITING

Revising Your Writing

With a partner, look at the article you wrote and revise it.

1. Content

    a. Did you use the information from the interview accurately? That is, do your statements have the same meaning as the statements in the transcript?

    b. If you used information of your own, did you state it accurately and clearly? Is the information all relevant?

2. Organization

    a. Does the title express the main idea of the article? Will it catch the readers' attention?

    b. Does each paragraph have one main idea? Does all the information in each paragraph reflect its main idea?

3. Cohesion and style

    Have you used transition words to unify your writing? Have you used too many transition words? (If you have, take some of them out.)

Editing Practice

Correcting Sentence Fragments

> A sentence fragment is a sentence that is incomplete. It can be a dependent clause that cannot stand alone. Check the appendix for a list of subordinating conjunctions that introduce dependent clauses.
>
> *Sentence fragment:*   When adults rode bikes.
> *Sentence fragment:*   Because they're expensive to manufacture.
>
> You can correct a sentence fragment that is a dependent clause by joining it to an independent clause. The dependent clause can go before or after the independent clause. Note that if the dependent clause precedes the independent clause, a comma usually follows it.
>
> *Correction:*   When adults rode bikes, they were usually three-speed touring bikes.
> *Correction:*   Racing bikes cost a lot because they're expensive to manufacture.

A. Correct these sentence fragments. Don't forget to use a comma if you put the dependent clause before the independent clause.

1. Because it is less expensive.

    _____

    _____

2. When you own a car.

    _____

    _____

3. If you can't afford insurance.

    _____

    _____

4. Since the subway system is very reliable.

_____

_____

5. So that they can go as fast uphill as they can on level ground.

_____

_____

6. Although taking public transportation can save you a lot of money.

_____

_____

B. Edit this paragraph for sentence fragments.

These lightweight bicycles offer several advantages. Many people choose them over three-speeds. Because they are usually well made and of high-quality materials. The different gears allow the rider to work at a steady rate. So that he or she becomes less tired during long rides. In addition, although it costs a lot. A ten-speed racer shows that its owner is serious about cycling.

Editing Your Writing

Edit the article you wrote. You can also give it to a partner to check. Use this checklist.

GRAMMAR

1. Parts of speech
2. No sentence fragments

FORM

1. Paragraph form: indentation, margins, capitalization
2. Punctuation of dependent clauses
3. Spelling

Writing the Second Draft

After you edit your article, rewrite it neatly, using good handwriting and correct form.

PART FOUR

COMMUNICATING THROUGH WRITING

Give your article to your teacher for comments.

Sharing

In small groups, read your articles. What advantages or disadvantages of public transportation did you describe that were not in the interview? How do you feel about public transportation in the area where you live?

Using Feedback

Look at your teacher's comments about your article. If you don't understand something, ask about it.

Discuss these questions with your classmates.

1. Which writing did you enjoy more, the assignment for Chapter 5 or the assignment for this chapter?
2. In general, do you prefer writing about your life and ideas or about factual information that you have studied or looked up?
3. How are the two kinds of writing different? How are they similar?
4. What can you learn by practicing each kind of writing?

Developing Your Skills

A. Find an advertisement in a magazine for a car. Bring it to class. With your classmates, discuss the positive features of the car in the ad. What are the possible disadvantages of owning this car? Write a paragraph summarizing your discussion.

B. Interview a friend who has a different way of getting to school than you do (driving, walking, taking the bus or subway, riding a bicycle). What are the reasons for his or her choice? Then, using your interview, write a paragraph about your friend's commute.

Developing Fluency

A. Write for fifteen minutes about your commute to school or any other place you go every day. How do you feel about this trip? Is it boring? Interesting? What sights do you see? Do you see the same people each time?

B. Compare your experiences using public transportation in your culture with those in the city you live in now. Share your work with a partner.

C. Write about whatever comes to mind.

7

NORTH AMERICA: THE LAND AND THE PEOPLE

GETTING READY TO WRITE

Exploring Ideas

Interviewing Someone

A. A great majority of the populations of the United States and Canada is made up of immigrants or descendants of immigrants. Look at this picture of immigrants taking an oath of citzenship. In small groups, discuss these questions.

Becoming U.S. citizens

1. Why do people choose to immigrate to a new country?
2. What are some of the problems that immigrants face? Make a list of the problems.

_____

_____

_____

_____

_____

_____

3. If you were going to interview an immigrant, what questions would you like to ask him or her? Make a list of possible interview questions.

B. In this chapter, you are going to write about an immigrant—yourself, someone you know, someone in your class—or you can make up a story about someone in the picture on page 91. Work in pairs. Interview your partner using the interview questions you just wrote. On a separate page, take notes on your partner's answers. Then your partner will interview you and take notes on your answers. When your partner interviews you, you may answer as yourself, or you may pretend you are someone you know or someone in the picture on page 91.

C. Exchange notes. What else can you add to the notes your partner made?

Building Vocabulary

In your discussion you may have heard some words you don't understand, or you may find that you don't know the English word for some of the ideas you want to express. Find out the meaning of any words you don't understand and add them to the list below.

Nouns	Verbs	Adjectives
confusion	confuse	anxious
depression	depress	confusing
excitement	emigrate	depressed
homeland	excite	difficult
humiliation	humiliate	easy
native land	immigrate	exciting
refugee	thrill	homesick
thrill		humiliated
		lonely
_____	_____	lucky
	_____	thrilled
_____		upset
	_____	
_____		
	_____	_____
_____		
	_____	_____
_____		
		_____

Using Verbal Adjectives to Describe Feelings

Many of the verbs that describe emotions are verbal adjectives. Verbal adjectives take two forms. One form ends in *-ed*. It describes the person (or animal) that has a feeling. The other form ends in *-ing*. It describes the person, animal, or thing that creates a feeling.

Examples: Eva heard some *surprising* news.

She was *surprised* at the news.

Here is a list of some common verbal adjectives:

confused	excited	offended	thrilled
confusing	exciting	offending	thrilling
depressed	frightened	surprised	tired
depressing	frightening	surprising	tiring
disappointed	humiliated	terrified	
disappointing	humiliating	terrifying	

A. Look at these sentences. Draw an arrow from the adjective in italics to the noun phrase that it describes.

1. At first, the noise and crowds of the big city were *terrifying* to

   Ahmad.

2. Tran was *disappointed* when he couldn't find a job.

3. Living in a new country can be *frightening*.

4. Wilma was *surprised* that learning English was so easy.

B. Complete these sentences with adjective forms of the words below.

offend   thrill   depress
excite   tire   surprise

1. Tran was _____ by American customs.

2. Amara thought working full-time and studying was _____.

3. Alain was _____ and homesick when he first moved to the

   United States.

4. At first, Junko thought that life in New York was _____.

5. Most people think that flying is _____.

C. Complete these sentences with verbal adjectives. Talk about your true feelings. You may want to use verbal adjectives with the same meaning as *happy, sad,* or *scary.*

1. Life in the United States is _____.

2. I was _____ on the first day of class.

3. Leaving home is _____.

4. My friends and family were _____ when I left.

D. Write these sentences for your paragraphs, using verbal adjectives.

_____

_____

_____

_____

_____

_____

Organizing Ideas

Keeping to One Subject

When you write, you should be careful to keep to the subject. All of the information that you give should be closely related to the topic of your paragraph.

Read this paragraph. Does it contain any irrelevant information? Cross out any sentences that do not belong.

When Lee Kim first arrived in the United States from Korea, he was very frightened. Suddenly, he was entering a world that was almost totally incomprehensible to him. He was living in an apartment. He was unable to obtain information he needed. Lee could not read a street sign, ask a question, or understand directions. Lee's brother spoke English well. However, Lee's life changed for the better when he decided to go to Newton Community College to take English classes. This school is located on the corner of Broad Street and First Avenue.

Developing Ideas by Adding Details

> Be careful to write about one subject only and try to answer questions that the reader may have.

A. Read the following paragraph. Has the writer adequately developed his or her ideas? Do you still have questions about the topic?

> Juan Ordóñez had many dreams when he was young, so he decided to immigrate. He left his birthplace in 1986. When he first arrived in his new country, his life was very difficult. However, now he is much happier. Juan is glad that he decided to leave his homeland.

B. Write questions about the paragraph here. The answers to these questions are important details that would make the paragraph more interesting.

Example: What is Juan's new country?

1. _____
2. _____
3. _____
4. _____
5. _____

C. Working in small groups, make up answers to your questions, then rewrite the paragraph, using the new information. The result should be an interesting, well-developed paragraph.

Dividing a Composition into Paragraphs

> Now look at the notes you made for your story. Your story can have two or more paragraphs. For example, the first paragraph might be about the immigrant's life in his or her native country and the second paragraph about his or her new life. You might also choose to write one paragraph about what an immigrant's life was like upon first arriving and a second paragraph about how his or her life changed.
>
> Look at your notes and divide them into paragraphs. Is there any information that seems irrelevant? Is there any information you should add?

Writing Topic Sentences

> A good topic sentence should capture the reader's interest and explain what the paragraph is about.

A. Look at these topic sentences. Which ones do you like? Why? Can you add information to the ones you don't like in order to make them more interesting? Remember that there are several ways to make good topic sentences.

1. Basima never considered leaving her home before the summer of 1988.

2. Wai Fon Yu was born in Beijing.

3. Life in her native Colombia was not easy for Silvia.

4. Domingo is an immigrant from Spain.

5. His name is Walid.

B. Write a topic sentence for the first paragraph of your story.

Writing Concluding Sentences

> Although most immigrants face many problems, they often have hopes for the future. Your composition should end with a sentence that expresses such a hope.

Look at these concluding sentences. Which ones do you like the best? Why?

1. Marta is looking forward to a bright future now that her troubles are over.
2. José plans to live in Canada for the rest of his life.
3. Although Junpen is still sometimes homesick, she knows that her decision was the right one.
4. Mohammed is waiting for the day he can return home.

PART TWO

DEVELOPING WRITING SKILLS

Developing Cohesion and Style

Using Gerunds as Subjects

A gerund is a verbal noun. You can form a gerund by adding *-ing* to the simple form of the verb. (See the appendix for rules for spelling changes.) Gerunds are sometimes subjects of sentences.

Look at these sentences with gerunds.

Examples: *Moving to the United States* was the most exciting experience of Juan's life.

Becoming a Canadian citizen made Chomsak very proud.

Working as a garbage man made Gaetano sick.

A. Restate these sentences, making gerunds from the words in parentheses.

1. (Talk about politics) was forbidden in Teresa's country.

   _____

   _____

2. (Learn to live in a new culture) is difficult for anyone.

   _____

   _____

3. (Leave your homeland) is never easy.

   _____

   _____

4. (Live on welfare) was a humiliating experience for Samuel.

   _____

   _____

5. (Be away from his family) made Jaime very sad.

   _____

   _____

B. Complete these sentences with a gerund or a verb phrase.

1. Seeing the Statue of Liberty for the first time _____.

2. _____ made Marta very happy.

3. Going to night school and working _____.

4. Sending money home to her family _____.

5. _____ was easy for Katrina.

Using Gerunds and Infinitives in Parallel Constructions

> When you write it is important to use gerunds and infinitives in parallel constructions. The gerunds and infinitives in the following sentences are parallel.
>
> *Examples:*   *Working* during the day and *studying* at night made Miguel very tired.
>
> When I first arrived in Toronto, I liked *to walk* in beautiful parks and *listen* to people speak English.
>
> The gerunds and infinitives in these sentences are not parallel.
>
> *Examples:*   In our native country my family enjoyed *visit* relatives and *having* picnics in our orchard.
>
> *Visiting* new places and *to meet* new people always interested Shadi.

© PETER MENZEL/STOCK, BOSTON

Leaving friends and family is difficult.

The following paragraph includes some mistakes in the use of gerunds and infinitives. Find the mistakes and correct them.

A Difficult Decision

Decide to leave her country was very difficult for Berta. Unfortunately, in her native country she was unable to going to school or find a good job. When her husband suggested that they leave, she knew he was right. Visiting her friends and family for the last time was the hardest thing she ever had to do. She avoided calling and tell them of the decision for a long time. She was so lonely during her first few months abroad that she thought she would die. Berta feels comfortable in her new country now, but she has never stopped loving her country and to feel homesick for the people she left behind.

Using *Would* and *Used to*

When English speakers talk about past events they often use the simple past tense, but sometimes when they are talking about past habits they use *would + verb* or *used to + verb*.

Examples: When I was young, I *used to get up* early every morning.

When I was young, I *would get up* early every morning.

You can use *would* and *used to* to talk about repeated activities. However, for continuing states using verbs such as *have, think, live, believe,* and *own* you can use *used to* only.

Examples: Her grandfather *used to have* a long white beard.

She *used to think* that he was the oldest man in the world.

Remember that you cannot use *would* and *used to* for activities that happened only once or twice or states that continued for only a short time. In these cases you must use the simple past tense.

Examples: Anna started school when she was seven.

On the first day of school she was afraid because she thought that her mother was leaving her forever.

A. Complete these sentences in as many ways as possible. Some sentences can take only the simple past. Others can take the simple past or *used to*. Some can take the simple past, *would,* or *used to.*

1. Marta _____ used to _____ (live) in a small village in Ecuador.

2. When he was young, Alfonso _____ would _____ (visit) his grandmother every day.

3. Many immigrants _____ used to - would _____ (believe) that anyone could get rich very quickly in the United States.

4. When Greta was fifteen, she _____ used to - would _____ (come) to live in the United States.

5. In El Salvador, Teresa's family _____ used to - _____ (own) a large farm.

Many times students use *used to* too often in one paragraph. Good writers often begin with a sentence using *used to* and then continue with *would* or the simple past tense.

B. Read this paragraph. It sounds boring because the writer has used *used to* in every sentence.

From the time he was young, Salim had to work very hard. He used to get up early in the morning to study. After he finished studying, he used to go to work in his uncle's cheese factory. Then he used to go to school for morning classes. At lunchtime he used to deliver pastries for a local bakery. Then he used to go back to school. After school, he used to have to work at his uncle's factory for a few more hours. Despite all of his hard work, Salim used to be the best student in his class.

C. Rewrite the paragraph, changing *used to* to *would* or the simple past tense to make it more interesting.

D. Think about the paragraphs you are going to write about an immigrant. Write three or four sentences, using *used to* or *would*, that you could use in your composition.

Writing the First Draft

Write your composition using the topic sentence you wrote and the notes you made. Make your paragraphs interesting by adding details. Don't worry about grammar when you write the first draft. Write on every other line so you can revise your paragraph easily.

PART THREE

REVISING AND EDITING

Revising Your Writing

Adding Topic and Concluding Sentences and Omitting Irrelevant Information

A. The first paragraph of this composition needs a topic sentence, and the last paragraph needs a concluding sentence. Read the story and then add a topic sentence and a concluding sentence. Cross out any irrelevant information.

_____

_____

When Nu Phong was very young she lived in a small village in Vietnam with her parents and her brothers and sisters. Her parents were farmers. They grew rice and vegetables. Sometimes her parents would talk about the war but only a few soldiers came to Nu Phong's village, so her family felt safe. Nu Phong's older brother decided not to fight in the war. Then one day bombs began to fall on their village and many soldiers came to fight there. Nu Phong's parents died in the fighting. Nu Phong and her sister went to live with their grandmother in Saigon. One day when Nu Phong was fourteen their grandmother came and told them that they were going to go to the United States to live with their aunt.

At first, Nu Phong's life in the United States was very difficult. She went to an American high school and she felt very uncomfortable there. She went to John F. Kennedy High School in Houston, Texas. Learning English wasn't easy, and the other students were very different from her. Gradually, Nu Phong began to make friends, first with other foreign students and finally with some Americans. She learned to speak English well and became comfortable with the American way of life. Although Nu Phong still thought about her life in Vietnam, she didn't feel homesick anymore. Nu Phong's sister was still planning to return to Vietnam. Today Nu Phong is eighteen years old. When she graduates from high school, she plans to go to college to become a nurse.

_____

_____

_____

B. Look at the composition you wrote and revise it. Check it for these elements:

1. Content

   a. Is the information interesting?
   b. Does the composition answer most of the reader's questions? Is all the information relevant?

2. Organization

   a. Are the paragraphs organized according to time?
   b. Does your first paragraph have a good topic sentence?
   c. Does your last paragraph have a concluding sentence?

3. Cohesion and style

   a. Are your gerund and infinitive constructions parallel?
   b. Did you use verbal adjectives correctly?
   c. Did you use *used to* too often?

C. Discuss your revisions with another student.

Editing Practice

Punctuating Sentences with Transitions and Subordinating Conjunctions

Remember to use transition words to connect ideas in a paragraph. Don't over-use them, however. When transition words such as *first of all, finally, in addition,* and *also* come at the beginning of a sentence, put a comma after them.

Example: At first, Phong's life in the United States was very difficult.

Don't confuse subordinating conjunctions such as *when* and *because* with transition words. (See the appendix for lists of subordinating conjunctions and transition words.) Subordinating conjunctions connect dependent clauses and independent clauses within a *sentence.* Transition words connect ideas within an entire *paragraph,* in order to make it cohesive.

Subordinating conjunction: I was unhappy, *so* I wanted to go home.

Transition word: I couldn't speak English. I had no friends, and I was living in a terrible place. *Therefore,* I wanted to go home.

Edit this paragraph for correct punctuation around transition words and subordinating conjunctions.

May 14, 1981 was the most memorable day in my life. On that day, my family left our home in Iran to go to live in the United States. Although I was only eight years old I thought I knew what life would be like in America. Because I had seen many movies about life there I remember wondering if I would be able to have a horse and carry a gun. In addition even though my father kept telling me that we were going to be living in a big city, I still imagined myself in the "Wild West."

Editing Your Writing

Edit the composition you wrote. You can also give it to a partner to check. Use this checklist.

GRAMMAR

1. *Used to + verb; would + verb*
2. Parallel gerund and infinitive construction

FORM

1. Paragraph form: indentation, margins, capitalization
2. Punctuation of sentences with transition words and subordinating conjunctions
3. Spelling

Writing the Second Draft

After you edit your composition, rewrite it neatly, using good handwriting and correct form.

PART FOUR

COMMUNICATING THROUGH WRITING

Give your composition to your teacher for comments.

Sharing

Read your stories aloud in small groups. If you have written about yourself or someone from your country, you can bring in pictures of your family and your native country.

Using Feedback

Look at your teacher's comments. If you don't understand something, ask about it.

Look at all the compositions you have written so far. Chapters 1 and 3 were opinions. Chapters 2 and 4 were descriptions. Chapters 5 and 7 were narratives. Chapter 6 was about advantages and disadvantages.

1. What kind of writing do you enjoy the most? Why?
2. What kind of writing is the most difficult for you? Why?

Developing Your Skills

If you wrote your paragraph about yourself, or about one of the people in the picture on page 91, now interview a classmate. Write about his or her experiences. If you already wrote about someone else, write a paragraph about yourself.

Developing Fluency

A. Write for fifteen minutes on the feelings you had when you first arrived in North America. If you wish, exchange your work with a partner and compare your experiences.

B. Write for fifteen minutes on how you feel about life in North America right now. If you wish, choose a partner and discuss the differences between your feelings when you first arrived and your feelings now.

8

TASTES AND PREFERENCES

Mike Gallego

Corazón Aquino

PART ONE

GETTING READY TO WRITE

Exploring Ideas

Discussing Well-known People

A. Discuss the people in the photos. What do you know about them? Which of them do you like? Why do you like or not like them?

Julio Iglesias

Mother Teresa

Eddie Murphy

Princess Diana of Wales

Gabriel García Márquez

B. In this chapter you are going to write a composition comparing and contrasting two people. You will write about how they are similar and how they are different. Choose two people you are familiar with. It's best to choose two people who have the same profession or who have some common characteristics, but if you can't think of famous people you know much about, you can choose two friends. Use one or more of the following ways to develop ideas to write about.

1. Find a partner who knows about the two people you chose and discuss what you know with him or her.
2. In a small group, discuss the people you chose.
3. Look in a magazine, newspaper, or encyclopedia for more information.

C. Write about each of the two people you chose. Write as much as you can in ten minutes. Then, with the whole class, talk about what characteristics you can compare and contrast. Did you think about the following characteristics? Did you think of any other characteristics? Add them to the list.

appearance	reasons for success	_____	_____
contributions to society	style		
personal life	talent	_____	_____
personality			
		_____	_____

Building Vocabulary

A. Here are some traits you may be able to use in your comparisons. Did you use any others in the notes you wrote? If so, add them to the list.

Adjectives		
appealing	professional	_____
charismatic	radical	
cold	strong	_____
conservative	talented	
flamboyant	warm	_____
outgoing	weak	
popular	wholesome	_____
private		

B. When you write a composition, you have to be careful to use the correct forms of words that have different forms for different parts of speech. Complete this chart with the correct forms of these words. Use your dictionary if you wish.

Nouns	Verbs	Adjectives	Adverbs
_____	_____	conservative	_____
_____	contrast	contrasting	in contrast
difference	differ	_____	_____
excellence	excel	_____	_____
_____	idealize	_____	_____
popularity	_____	_____	_____
similarity	resemble	_____	similarly

Organizing Ideas

Listing Similarities and Differences

A. Look at this example of the similarities and differences between the popular performers Michael Jackson and Prince.

SIMILARITIES

blacks who have white as well as
   black audiences
don't give interviews
feminine appearance

DIFFERENCES

Michael
innocent
lives with parents
religious

Prince
outrageous costumes
songs not suitable for young
   people
flamboyant

Make a list of the similarities and differences between the two people you choose.

SIMILARITIES

_____

_____

_____

_____

_____

_____

_____

DIFFERENCES

_____

_____

_____

_____

_____

_____

_____

B. Look at your lists. Decide whether there are more similarities or differences between the two people. If there are more similarities, you will want to focus on the similarities in your composition, although you will also have to mention the differences. If there are more differences, you will focus on them.

C. Read this composition comparing Michael Jackson and Prince. Does the composition focus more on similarities or differences?

Outrageous Rock

Although the rock superstars Prince and Michael Jackson are similar in many ways, they also have important differences. Both singers are young black performers who are popular with white as well as black audiences. They are both charismatic singers with a feminine appearance. With the help of plastic surgery and heavy makeup, Michael has made his face more feminine looking. Prince also wears feminine make-up and sometimes dresses in feminine-looking clothes. In addition, both are very private people who refuse to do interviews.

Yet their differences are even more striking. While Michael is the innocent boy who doesn't want to grow up, Prince is outrageous and sexy. Michael lives with his parents and seems to lead a wholesome and religious personal life. He doesn't eat meat, makes commercials against the use of alcohol, and loves animals and Disneyland. Prince, on the other hand, is very flamboyant. He writes songs about subjects that most mothers wouldn't want their children to talk about. He used to perform in underwear and lace gloves. While Michael talks about ideal love, Prince sings about having a good time. Although both singers unite opposites—black and white, feminine and masculine—Michael seems much more innocent in his performances.

Writing Topic Sentences

A. Look at the first sentence of the preceding composition. It is the topic sentence of the whole composition and identifies the two people the writer is comparing. Which part focuses on the similarities? Which part focuses on the differences?

B. Tell whether the focus of the compositions with these topic sentences is on similarities or differences.

1. There were more similarities than differences between Presidents John F. Kennedy and Jimmy Carter, even though most American people feel very differently about them. _____

2. There are many important differences between baseball stars Dave Winfield and Don Mattingly; however, their similarities are even more striking. _____

C. Write a topic sentence for your paragraph. You can use structures similar to the ones just given.

_____

_____

Analyzing the Organization of a Composition

Answer these questions about the organization of the composition about Michael Jackson and Prince.

1. Which paragraph describes the similarities? Which one describes the differences? What is the topic sentence of the second paragraph?
2. Look at these vocabulary items. Which ones does the writer use to show similarities? Which ones show differences?

   both   while   on the other hand   more

3. What transitional expressions does the writer use when mentioning additional similarities or differences?
4. Does the writer use any comparative structures (*more + adjective, adjective + -er*)?

PART TWO

DEVELOPING WRITING SKILLS

Developing Cohesion and Style

Using *Both* in Comparisons

There are several different ways to use *both* in a sentence that shows similarities.

1. Before nouns:

    Examples: Both singers are young black performers.

    Both Mr. Jackson and Prince are young black performers.

2. As a pronoun:

    Examples: Both are young black performers.

3. With verbs (note the position of *both* with different types of verbs):

    Examples: They are both young black performers. (*Both* follows the verb *be*.)

    They have both been popular with white audiences. (*Both* follows the first auxiliary verb.)

    They both dress flamboyantly. (*Both* goes before one-word verbs except *be*.)

Using *Neither* in Comparisons

You can use *neither* in several different ways to show negative similarities. Note that *neither* is singular.

1. As a pronoun:

    Examples: Neither likes to give interviews.

    Neither of the singers likes to give interviews.

2. Before a singular noun:

    Example: Neither singer likes to give interviews.

3. With *nor:*

    Example: Neither Michael nor Prince likes to give interviews.

Stevie Wonder and Boy George

A. Write sentences about the picture above. Use the phrases given and *neither* or *both*.

1. wearing a hat _____

   _____

2. singing _____

   _____

3. look _____

   _____

4. using microphones _____

   _____

5. sitting _____

   _____

6. playing the guitar _____

   _____

B. Write two sentences about the similarities between the two people you chose. Use *neither* or *both*.

1. _____

   _____

2. _____

   _____

Using *While* to Show Contrast

You can use *while* in a sentence that shows differences. Note that you can use *while* before either clause of the sentence.

Examples: While Michael talks about ideal love, Prince sings about having a good time.

Michael talks about ideal love, while Prince sings about having a good time.

Look at these lists showing the differences between former presidents Kennedy and Reagan, and write sentences with *while*.

<u>Kennedy</u>	<u>Reagan</u>
was the youngest president in the history of the United States	was 73 years old at the beginning of his second term
was one of the most popular presidents outside the United States	made many decisions that weren't popular abroad
came from a rich and influential family	was from a middle-class family and was an actor most of his life
died soon after Lee Harvey Oswald shot him in Dallas	recovered quickly from the wounds caused by an attempted assassination
wanted to increase aid to the poor	tried to cut many of the programs that served the poor

Using Expressions of Contrast: *In Contrast* and *On the Other Hand*

You can use *in contrast* or *on the other hand* to show differences. These expressions have similar meanings and you should use them after descriptions that are longer than one sentence. Good stylists often put the expressions after the subject. Use commas to separate them from the rest of the sentences.

Examples: Prince, on the other hand, is more flamboyant.

Prince, in contrast, is more flamboyant.

In the following sentences, insert *in addition* to show additional similar information. Insert *in contrast* or *on the other hand* to show contrasting information.

1. Boy George is a British singer. He and his band Culture Club didn't become popular for a long time. Michael Jackson is an American who has been a popular singer since he was a child.

2. Boy George often dresses in feminine-looking clothes and uses heavy makeup. He wears a lot of jewelry and sometimes wears women's wigs.

3. Some writers say that Michael Jackson is an "eternal boy." He is a youthful singer who doesn't want to grow up. Boy George is cynical and wise to the ways of the world.

4. Boy George and Michael Jackson both combine masculine and feminine characteristics. They both sing songs that are popular with many different audiences.

Writing the First Draft

Write your composition using the organization you came up with at the beginning of this chapter. Use *both* and *neither* to show similarities. Use *while, in contrast,* or *on the other hand* to show differences. You can also use *however* and *although* to show contrast. Write on every other line so you can revise your paragraph easily.

PART THREE

REVISING AND EDITING

Revising Your Writing

Organizing Sentences into Paragraphs

A. Following are two topic sentences for a short composition of two paragraphs about the American presidents John F. Kennedy and Jimmy Carter. Complete both paragraphs by filling in the sentences from page 118; put the sentences that describe differences in the first paragraph and the ones that describe similarities in the second paragraph. Add *both, neither, while,* and *in contrast* to the sentences.

John F. Kennedy

Jimmy Carter

More Alike Than Different?

There were more similarities than differences between Presidents John F. Kennedy and Jimmy Carter, even though many Americans feel very differently about them. _____

_____

_____

_____

_____

_____

_____

_____

_____

These two presidents, however, shared some of the same ideals and accomplishments. _____

_____

_____

_____

_____

_____

_____

_____

_____

1. They entered the presidency as outsiders—Carter because he was a Southerner and Kennedy because he was a Catholic.
2. Almost all Americans born before 1950 can remember what they were doing when they heard the news about Kennedy's assassination, and most watched his funeral with great sorrow and missed this very popular president.
3. They shared the ideal of a world of peace and worked with the Russians to limit nuclear arms.
4. They were Democrats who narrowly defeated their Republican opponents.
5. Few people felt bad when Jimmy Carter left office. They thought he was a weak president and many blamed him when Iran held U.S. citizens hostage.
6. President Kennedy fought for civil rights for all races and President Carter fought for human rights throughout the world.
7. President Kennedy established an arms control aggreement and President Carter successfully negotiated a peace agreement between Israel and Egypt.
8. Although President Johnson was able to carry out most of Kennedy's programs after his death, Carter and Kennedy had trouble working with Congress.

B. Look at the composition you wrote and revise it. Check it for these elements:

1. Content

   a. Is the information interesting?
   b. Is the information accurate?

2. Organization

   a. Does the topic sentence mention both similarities and differences even though it focuses on one or the other?
   b. Does one paragraph deal with differences and one with similarities?

3. Cohesion and style
   Did you use such expressions as *both, neither, in contrast, on the other hand,* and *while?*

C. Discuss your revisions with another student.

Editing Practice

Using Comparatives and Superlatives

When making comparisons between two things or people, either use *more* or *less* before the adjective that describes the point of comparison or add *-er* to the end of the adjective. In general, one-syllable adjectives take the *-er* ending, two-syllable adjectives can take either the *-er* ending or the words *more* or *less,* and adjectives with more than two syllables always take *more* or *less.*

With two-syllable adjectives that end in *-y,* change the *y* to *i* before adding *-est.* For example, *happy* becomes *happiest.*

$$\text{X is} \left\{ \begin{array}{l} adjective + \text{-er} \\ more \, (less) + adjective \end{array} \right\} \text{ than Y.}$$

Examples: Kennedy was younger than Reagan when he became president.

Michael Jackson is more religious than Prince.

Prince is less wholesome than Michael Jackson.

In describing a thing or person that has the greatest or least degree of a quality, precede the adjective with *most* or *least* or add the ending *-est,* depending on the number of syllables.

$$\text{X is the} \left\{ \begin{array}{l} adjective + \text{-est} \\ most \, (least) + adjective \end{array} \right\} \text{ of or in a group.}$$

Examples: Kennedy was the youngest president in the history of the United States.

Prince is one of the most outrageous personalities in contemporary music.

Michael Jackson is one of the least egotistical personalities of all the popular singers I can think of.

A. Write sentences using the comparative and superlative forms of the adjectives in parentheses. Base your answers on information from the text, outside sources, or your own opinions.

1. Prince is _____ (flamboyant) than Michael Jackson.

2. Sting is _____ (popular) internationally than Michael Jackson.

3. Michael Jackson is one of the _____ (shy) rock performers offstage.

4. _____ (fill in any rock performer's name) is _____ (outrageous) in appearance than Boy George.

5. Michael Jackson's lifestyle appears to be _____ (wholesome) than _____ (fill in any rock performer's name).

6. Sting's song lyrics are among the _____ (political) of all contemporary music performers.

B. Edit this paragraph for errors in the use of comparatives and superlatives.

Although there are some similarities between baseball stars Dave Winfield and Don Mattingly, even more interestinger are their similarities. Winfield has been playing professional baseball for years. At six feet, six

Dave Winfield (left)
receives congratulations
from Don Mattingly after
hitting a home run.

© JEFF REINKING/WIDE WORLD PHOTOS

inches, he is more tall than Mattingly, and he makes one of the highester salaries among U.S. baseball players. People say he also has one of the large egos! Mattingly, on the other hand, is younger Winfield. People call him the Kid. He has a more pleasanter personality than Winfield. Being just under 6 feet, he's a bit short than Winfield, and makes one-tenth of his salary.

Editing Your Writing

Edit the composition you wrote. You can also give it to a partner to check. Use this checklist.

> GRAMMAR
>
> Comparatives and superlatives
>
> FORM
> 1. Paragraph form: indentation, margins, capitalization
> 2. Punctuation of sentences with expressions of contrast (*in contrast, on the other hand, while*)
> 3. Spelling

Writing the Second Draft

After you edit your composition, rewrite it neatly, using good handwriting and correct form.

PART FOUR

COMMUNICATING THROUGH WRITING

Give your composition to your teacher for comments.

Sharing

As a class, put together a collection of your best writing. Each student will submit a composition for the collection. Look at the compositions you have written so far and choose the one you like the best or write another story, poem, or composition. Type or write your selection neatly. Your teacher will collect the pieces of writing.

Using Feedback

Look at your teacher's comments carefully. If you don't understand something, ask about it.

Look at all the compositions you have written so far. Is there one kind of grammar mistake you often make? Look in your grammar book for an explanation and exercises on the grammatical structure and practice using the structure correctly.

Developing Your Skills

A. Find a comparison of two people or things in a magazine article. Note the words and expressions the writer uses in the comparison. Is he or she focusing mainly on differences or similarities?

B. Write a paragraph comparing two teachers that you have had. Choose two that taught the same subject, if possible. Give your paragraph to a partner to read.

Developing Fluency

A. Write a comparison of two actors/actresses, pop singers, politicians, or athletes from your country or culture. Emphasize their differences. Write for fifteen minutes.

B. Write on the same subject as you did for Activity A above, but this time, emphasize similarities. Again, write for fifteen minutes.

C. Choose a topic you would like your partner to write about in his or her journal. Write about the topic your partner chooses. Then exchange journals and comment on each other's work.

9

THE SKY ABOVE US

GETTING READY TO WRITE

Exploring Ideas

Obtaining Information from Charts and Graphs

Students often have to use material written by others in order to get accurate information that they need to write about certain subjects. This is especially true in the physical and social sciences. Information in these areas is often presented in charts and tables.

In this chapter, you will practice getting information from charts and tables for writing a paragraph about one of the planets.

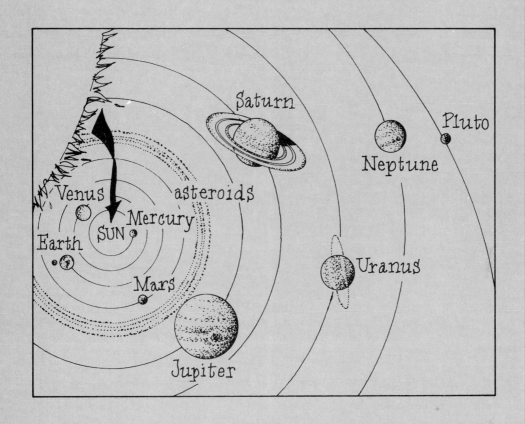

A. Look at the picture above and the charts and tables on pages 126–128. Answer the following questions.

1. Which planet is the largest?
2. Which planet is the farthest from the sun?
3. Which planet has the most moons?
4. Which planet rotates the most slowly?
5. Which planet has the fastest rotation?
6. How many moons does Saturn have?
7. When was Uranus discovered?
8. Which planets have been visited by spacecraft?
9. What is Mars' atmosphere made of?
10. What is an interesting feature of Jupiter?
11. Who discovered Pluto?
12. What do some people call Venus?
13. Which planets have rings?

	Average Temperature	Diameter (in miles)	Number of Moons
Mercury	950°F on sunny side; −350°F on dark side	3,030	0
Venus	800°F	7,520	0
Earth	59°F	7,926	1
Mars	extremes are 65°F to −190°F	4,200	2
Jupiter	19,300°F	88,800	16
Saturn	−228°F in atmosphere	74,500	23
Uranus	−270°F	32,000	15
Neptune	−330°F	30,200	2
Pluto	no information	1,000	1

	Rotation	Distance from Sun (millions of miles)	Revolution Around Sun
Mercury	58.6 days	35.9	88 days
Venus	243 days	67.2	224.7 days
Earth	23:56 hrs./mins.	92.9	365.25 days
Mars	24:37 hrs./mins.	141.6	686 days
Jupiter	9:55 hrs./mins.	483.6	11.9 years
Saturn	10:39 hrs./mins.	886.7	29.5 years
Uranus	17 hrs.	1783.2	84 years
Neptune	17.7 hrs.	2798.9	164.89 years
Pluto	6.39 days	3666.2	247.7 years

	Composition of Atmosphere	Features
Mercury	little or no atmosphere	craters like the moon
Venus	carbon dioxide	220-m.p.h. winds
Earth	nitrogen, oxygen	
Mars	carbon dioxide, nitrogen, argon, oxygen	bright red color; polar ice caps; volcanoes
Jupiter	hydrogen, helium, water, ammonia, methane	Great Red Spot, 25,000 miles long; one ring
Saturn	hydrogen, helium	huge system of rings of rock and ice
Uranus	hydrogen, helium, methane	11 rings, ocean of superheated water
Neptune	hydrogen, helium, methane	cloudy, fluid atmosphere and rocky core
Pluto	no information	consists mainly of water ice with a crust of methane ice

	Planet Discovery	Exploration
Mercury		in 1975 Mariner 10 found magnetic field, which surprised scientists
Venus		Soviet Spacecraft Venera 8 landed on Venus in 1972, sent information for one hour, was then destroyed by heat
Mars		Viking spacecraft landed in 1975, analyzed soil samples
Jupiter		Pioneers 10 and 11 sent back photographs in 1975; Voyagers 1 and 2 sent back moving pictures in 1979
Saturn		Pioneer 11, 1979
Uranus	Sir William Herschel, 1781	Voyager 2 sent back information in 1986
Neptune	Gottfried Galle, 1846	Voyager 2 will visit in 1989
Pluto	C. W. Tombaugh, 1930	

	Other Information
Venus	also known as the Morning Star or Evening Star; rotates from west to east
Mercury	no atmosphere
Mars	changes color; scientists believe it has seasons
Jupiter	Great Red Spot (cloud system); composition like the sun's
Saturn	huge cloud system, mostly white ammonia clouds
Uranus	greenish glow
Neptune	bluish color; partial rings (arcs) that do not completely circle the planet; discovered because astronomers wanted to know why Uranus sometimes speeded up and at other times slowed down
Pluto	irregular orbit; is sometimes the eighth planet, but normally the ninth planet, from the sun

B. In this chapter you are going to write a paragraph describing a planet. Select a planet other than Earth or Uranus. Study the information about the planet given on the preceding pages and complete this chart with the correct information. You may not be able to find information for every category for each planet.

Name: _____

Size: _____

Distance from the sun: _____

Composition: _____

Rotation: _____

Revolution around the sun: _____

Discovered: _____

Exploration: _____

_____

Moons: _____

Interesting features: _____

_____

Other information: _____

_____

_____

Building Vocabulary

A. In filling out the preceding chart, you may have found that you don't know the English words for some of the concepts you want to express. Find the words you need and add them to the list below.

Nouns	Verbs	Adjectives
atmosphere	be composed of	inhabited
composition	discover	uninhabited
diameter	explore	_____
discover	inhabit	_____
discovery	revolve	_____
exploration	rotate	_____
orbit	_____	_____
revolution	_____	_____
rotation		
_____	_____	_____
_____	_____	_____
_____	_____	_____
_____	_____	_____
_____	_____	

B. In writing about a planet, you will probably need to use expressions to describe the planet's position, movements, and composition. What other expressions can you think of? Add them to the list.

LOCATION/MOTION

is surrounded by
lies between
passes by / passes close to
revolves around
rotates around

_____

COMPOSITION

is composed of
is made of
was formed by

_____

_____

Examples: The atmosphere of Saturn is composed of hydrogen and helium.

Two moons revolve around Mars.

Organizing Ideas

Making Comparisons

> One way to make your paragraph more interesting is to tell the reader how the planet you are writing about is different from the earth or the other planets.

A. Look at your notes. Compare the planet you chose to Earth. Answer these questions.

1. Is it very much larger or smaller?
2. Does it have a much longer or shorter period of rotation or revolution?
3. Is it much hotter or colder?
4. Is it much farther from the sun?

B. Think of some other ways to compare Earth and the planet you chose.

_____

_____

_____

_____

C. Compare the planet you chose to the other planets. Answer these questions.

1. Is it the largest or one of the largest? The smallest or one of the smallest?
2. Is its atmosphere very different from the others?
3. Do scientists know a lot more or less about it than they do about other planets?

D. Finally, think of some other ways to compare your planet to the others in the solar system. Make notes of any interesting comparisons you have found. Remember, the greater the difference, the more interesting your comparison will be.

_____

_____

_____

_____

Ordering Information in a Paragraph

> A paragraph like the kind you will write in this chapter does not present information in any particular order. However, it is important to keep related information together.

A. These topics are a list of the information given in the following paragraph. Read the paragraph. Then number the facts according to the order in which they are presented.

_____ Exploration

_____ Discovery

_____ Length of year, day

_____ Composition of atmosphere

_____ Position

_____ Features

Uranus, the seventh planet in the solar system, lies between the planets of Saturn and Neptune. Uranus's orbit is much larger than earth's. It takes this planet 84 earth-years to complete its trip around the sun. However, a day on Uranus is shorter than a day on Earth. It lasts only 17 hours. Uranus was discovered in 1781 by the British astronomer Sir William Herschel. In 1986, the Voyager 2 spaceship passed by Uranus and took pictures; before that, not much had been learned about the planet. Scientific studies have now shown that its atmosphere is composed of hydrogen, helium, and methane and has a temperature of approximately $-270°F$. It has deep oceans of very hot water and a bright glow. The Voyager 2 pictures also showed that Uranus has eleven rings and fifteen moons. Scientists hope to learn much more about this distant planet in the future.

B. Look at the notes for your paragraph and put them in the order you wish to state them.

PART TWO

DEVELOPING WRITING SKILLS
Developing Cohesion and Style

Using the Passive Voice

All passive voice sentences contain a form of *be* + *past participle of the main verb*. The passive voice is often used in scientific and technical writing. It has two main uses.

1. It is used to emphasize or focus on the person or thing acted upon rather than the person or thing that performed the action of the main verb.

   Examples: (active voice) Sir William Herschel discovered Uranus.

   (passive voice) Uranus was discovered by Sir William Herschel.

   (active voice) The moon orbits the earth.

   (passive voice) The earth is orbited by the moon.

Note that the agent or doer of the action is introduced with *by*.

2. The passive voice is used when the person or thing that performs that action of the verb in the active voice is unknown or unimportant.

   Examples: (active voice) Scientists have discovered that there is no water on the moon.

   (passive voice) It has been discovered that there is no water on the moon.

   (active voice) People do not inhabit the other planets in our solar system.

   (passive voice) The other planets in our solar system are uninhabited.

A view of the moon

A. Complete the following paragraph with the appropriate passive or active forms of the verbs in parentheses. Don't forget to put the verb in the correct tense.

The Moon

The moon _____ (orbit) the earth the way the earth _____
                  1   2
(orbit) the sun. Scientists believe that it _____ (form) at about the
                                                   3
same time as the earth. They now know that it _____ (make up of)
                                                         4
many of the same materials. But scientists _____ (find) that the
                                                    5
moon is different from the earth in many ways. For example, the moon
_____ (have) no atmosphere to carry sound, so no matter what
           6
_____ (happen) no sound _____ (hear). Without an atmo-
          7   8
sphere, water _____ (disappear) into space. That is why no water
                      9
can _____ (find) on the surface of the moon, although some water
              10
_____ (trap) inside rocks. Without water there can _____
          11   12
(be) no weather. So if you go to the moon, you will never _____
                                                                              13
(see) a cloud, _____ (get) wet in a rainstorm, or _____
                      14   15
(feel) the wind blow.

B. Look at the notes you made for your paragraph. Write three sentences in the passive voice about your planet based on your notes. Show your sentences to a classmate. Can he or she find any errors?

Varying Word Order: *With + Noun Phrase*

> You can make your paragraph more interesting by changing the order of the elements in your sentence. For example, you can occasionally begin a sentence with a clause using *with + noun phrase.*
>
> *Example:*   With a diameter of 88,800 miles, Jupiter is the largest planet in the solar system.
>
> When you use this type of construction, you must make sure that the noun modified follows *with + noun phrase* directly. The following sentence is incorrect: *With a temperature of 900°F, no life could survive on Venus.* The subject (*no*) *life* is not what has a temperature of 900°F. The correct sentence would read: *With a temperature of 900°F, Venus is much too hot for life to survive.*

A. Match the clauses in Column A with the clauses in Column B.

	A		**B**
1.	_____ With its beautiful rings,	a.	Mars has interested astronomers for a long time.
2.	_____ With a diameter of only 3,000 miles,	b.	Venus could not support life.
3.	_____ With a daytime temperature of 800°F,	c.	Saturn is the most spectacular planet in the solar system.
4.	_____ With its bright red color and changing surface features,	d.	Mercury is the smallest planet in the solar system.

B. Write a sentence about your planet using *with + noun phrase.*

_____

_____

Using *Unlike + Noun Phrase* to Show Contrast

> Another way to make your paragraph more interesting is to begin a sentence by comparing the planet you are writing about to Earth or to the other planets.
>
> *Examples:*   *Unlike all the other planets,* Venus rotates from west to east.
>
>   *Unlike Earth,* Mercury has no atmosphere.

Complete each of the following sentences.

1. Unlike Earth, Mars _____
    _____.

2. Unlike Uranus and Neptune, Pluto _____
    _____.

3. Unlike Earth, Jupiter _____
    _____.

4. Unlike the other planets, Mercury _____
    _____.

Giving Reasons with *Because of* + *Noun Phrase* and *Because* + *Clause*

You have already learned how to use *because* to connect two clauses.

Example: No one can live on Mercury *because* it is very hot.

The phrase *because of* is used with a noun phrase rather than a clause.

Example: No one can live on Mercury *because of* its high temperature.

Note that *because* is followed by a subject and a verb, but *because of* is followed by a noun.

  Both *because* and *because of* can be used in the middle or at the beginning of a sentence. When you begin a sentence in the second way you must remember to put a comma after the first clause or phrase.

Examples: Pluto is sometimes the eighth planet in the solar system because it has an irregular orbit.

Because it has an irregular orbit, Pluto is sometimes the eighth planet in the solar system.

Pluto is sometimes the eighth planet in the solar system because of its irregular orbit.

Because of its irregular orbit, Pluto is sometimes the eighth planet in the solar system.

A. Add *because of* or *because* to the phrases and clauses in Column A. Then match the terms in Column A and Column B to make logical sentences.

	A		**B**
1.	_____ its irregular orbit,	a.	the sun holds all the planets in orbit.
2.	_____ its distance from the sun,	b.	Mercury has no atmosphere.
		c.	Pluto is extremely cold.
3.	_____ a desire to learn more about the solar system,	d.	Pluto is sometimes the eighth planet in the solar system.
		e.	many spaceships have been launched.
4.	_____ our need for oxygen,	f.	Mars has always interested sky-watchers.
5.	_____ it is close to Earth,		
6.	_____ its large size,	g.	human beings could not live on Mars.
7.	_____ it is small in size,		

B. Write a sentence about your planet using *because* or *because of.*

_____

_____

Writing the First Draft

Write your paragraph using the chart you filled out in Part One. Use the passive voice when necessary. Try to compare your planet with Earth or the other planets. Make your paragraph more interesting by varying the sentence structure with *unlike + noun phrase* and *with + noun phrase*. Give reasons with *because* or *because of.* Write on every other line so you can revise your paragraph easily.

PART THREE

REVISING AND EDITING

Revising Your Writing

A. Look at your paragraph and check it for these elements:

1. Content

    a. Is your information accurate?
    b. Have you made interesting comparisons?

2. Organization

    Is the information organized in a logical way?

3. Cohesion and style

   a. Did you use the passive voice when necessary?
   b. Did you vary sentence structure by moving some clauses to the beginning?
   c. Did you use *with, unlike,* or *because of* + *noun phrase* correctly?
   d. Did you use *because* + *noun* correctly?

B. With a partner, look at the paragraph you wrote and revise it.

Editing Practice

Using the Passive Voice

Edit this paragraph for errors in the use of the passive voice, and rewrite it correctly.

Uranus

Uranus, the seventh planet in the solar system, locates between the planets of Saturn and Neptune. Uranus's orbit is much larger than Earth's. This planet's trip around the sun is taked in 84 earth-years. However, a day on Uranus is shorter than a day on earth. It lasts only 17 hours. Uranus be discovered in 1781 by the British astronomer Sir William Herschel. In 1986 the Voyager 2 spaceship was passed by Uranus and took pictures; before that, not much had learned about its composition. Scientific studies have now been shown that its atmosphere is composing of hydrogen, helium, and methane and has a temperature of approximately −270°F. It has deep oceans of very hot water and a bright glow. The Voyager 2 pictures also show that Uranus has eleven rings and fifteen moons. Scientists hope to learn much more about this distant planet in the future.

Editing Your Writing

Edit the paragraph you wrote. You can also give it to a partner to check. Use this checklist.

GRAMMAR

The passive voice

FORM

1. Paragraph form: indentation, margins, capitalization
2. Punctuation of sentences with *with, unlike,* or *because of* + *noun phrase* and *because* + *clause*
3. Spelling

Writing the Second Draft

After you edit your paragraph, rewrite it neatly, using good handwriting and correct form.

PART FOUR

COMMUNICATING THROUGH WRITING

Sharing

Give your composition to your teacher for comments.

The class should try to find pictures of the planets and then put them on a bulletin board with the paragraphs from the class.

Using Feedback

Look at your teacher's comments. If you don't understand something, ask about it. Look back at your other compositions. What do you have the most difficulty with? What do you do best?

1. generating ideas
2. organizing your ideas
3. grammar
4. finding errors

Developing Your Skills

A. Find a description of how an object (for example, a tool or an appliance) is used. Appliance or user's manuals (written material that comes with the product when you buy it) are good sources of this kind of writing. Note the use of the passive voice. Is it used a lot? A little? Are the instructions generally clear? Why or why not?

B. Imagine that your classmate is from another planet and has never seen an object that you use every day—for example, a telephone or a pencil. Write a paragraph describing it to him or her. Then exchange paragraphs.

Developing Fluency

A. Write a paragraph describing a full moon to a blind person. Hint: Think about how the things you *see* would *feel* if you could touch them.

B. Write for fifteen minutes on the following topic: Would you like to travel in space? Why or why not?

MEDICINE, MYTHS, AND MAGIC

GETTING READY TO WRITE

Exploring Ideas

Discussing Medical Issues

Look at the pictures and discuss these questions.

1. What do you know about the handicaps that the children have?
2. Do you know anyone with a serious handicap?
3. How do parents of severely handicapped children feel?
4. What kind of lives do you think children with severe handicaps lead?

> In this chapter you are going to write an answer to this question: "Some children are born with severe mental handicaps. Should parents and doctors of these children be allowed to let them die?"
>
> Your answer to this question will depend on what you know from personal experience or from your reading.

Children with Down's syndrome have moderate to severe mental retardation and slow physical development. Most do not live past the age of 35.

Some children are born with severe brain damage. Many live their lives with a mental age lower than one year.

Although some people with cerebral palsy are mentally retarded, many have normal intelligence. They have problems with muscle control and may also be blind or deaf.

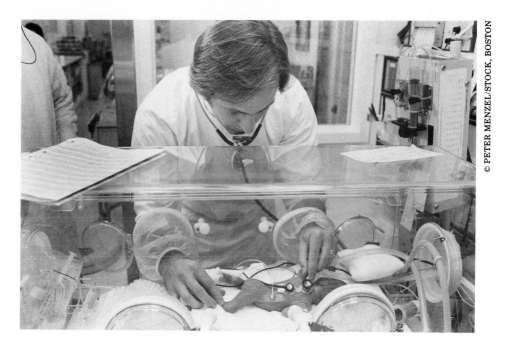

Baby in an intensive-care nursery

A. Read these accounts by parents of children with severe mental handicaps.

My daughter Tracy was born prematurely. A few days after her birth, a blood hemmorrhage (a heavy flow of blood) destroyed part of her brain. The doctors said that she would be severely mentally retarded and would probably not walk or talk. With the help of our doctor, we decided that if her heart should fail, the doctors should not try to bring her back to life. But the hospital said this was not our decision to make, because the law requires them to keep all babies alive, even if their brains are severely damaged.

So Tracy stayed in the hospital for six months, at a cost of $90,000. She was on different machines and had several operations. It became difficult for me to visit her in the hospital without feeling sick because it seemed to me that they were torturing her. Now she is home with us. We love her very much, but she is not developing mentally and we feel that she will not be able to lead a real life. We still feel it would have been better to let her die a natural death instead of keeping her alive artificially.

*   *   *

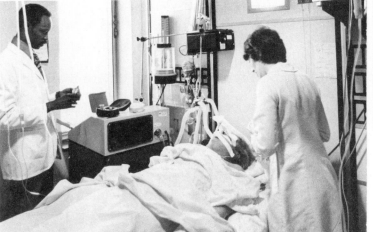

Patient on life-support machines

3. Because each situation is different, the family and doctors of a patient on a life-support system should decide whether or not to remove the person from the machines.
4. While many sick people in the world are dying because they don't have the money for proper medical care, we spend millions of dollars to keep people with no hope of recovery on life-support machines. We should use this money to help the people with a chance of recovery.

B. Write the first few sentences for your composition. State your opinion clearly and focus it on one particular idea.

_____

_____

_____

_____

_____

Supporting an Argument with Examples

> Good writers support their opinions with examples. You can use examples from your own experience or from articles you have read.

A. What example is given in this composition? Underline it.

The Right to Choose

People on life-support machines are all different and in different situations. For that and other reasons, I believe the family and doctor of the patient on a life-support machine should be able to decide whether to remove the person from the machine or not. If the person on the machine is able to participate in the decision, he or she should definitely have the right to choose.

With modern technology, it is very difficult to determine what is real life and what is artificial life. Is a person who is breathing with the help of a machine but whose brain is dead really alive or not? No one can say for sure because each individual situation is different.

I recently saw a program on T.V. that illustrates how the government's interference causes great suffering. A machine was breathing for a man who was dying of cancer and he wanted to be removed from it. He said, "I want to live, but not tied to a machine." When he tried to turn off the machine himself, the doctors tied his hands to the bed because they thought the government would sue them if the man died. I think it is wrong to ignore the patient's wishes.

If a patient is still breathing with the help of machines but has no hope of recovery, the family of the patient may suffer greatly. Not only do they have problems mentally and psychologically because of the stress of such a situation, but they may be forced to spend huge amounts of money on these expensive machines. The same amount of money could save lives of people in other situations. The family may be financially ruined and still the patient has no hope.

I am against the use of life-support systems against the will of a patient, and his or her family and doctor. We live in a country where people have individual rights. One of these rights is the right to die with dignity.

B. Think of examples you can use to support your argument. You can use examples from your own experience or from one of the accounts given earlier in this chapter.

DEVELOPING WRITING SKILLS

Developing Cohesion and Style

Using Restrictive Adjective Clauses

> Restrictive adjective clauses are often used to identify people, places, and things in writing. Commas are not used with restrictive clauses.
>
> *Examples:*   A machine was breathing for a man *who was dying of cancer.*
>
> We live in a country *where people have individual rights.*
>
> A machine *that breathed for her* was keeping her alive.

Complete these sentences with restrictive adjective clauses beginning with *who, that, where,* or *when.*

1. I know a man _____

2. A hospital is a place _____

3. People should be kept alive with machines _____
    _____

4. There are children _____

5. The child had a doctor _____

6. There are special hospital departments _____
    _____

Using Transitions and Giving Examples

The example from the composition "The Right to Choose" was introduced with this sentence:

> I recently saw a program on T.V. that illustrates how the government's interference causes great suffering.

That sentence is a transition sentence. It shows the purpose of the example. When you give an example, you can introduce it with expressions such as these:

_____ is a story/program/person that illustrates _____.

An example of _____ is _____.

_____ is an example of _____.

_____ shows _____.

I once knew _____.

A. Match these parts of sentences.

1. _____ The way in which my grand-mother approached her death
2. _____ I once knew a handicapped person
3. _____ The story of a neighbor of mine
4. _____ This story of a friend of my mother's shows

a. is an example of how the government can protect the rights of a handicapped child.

b. how difficult it is to raise a brain-damaged child.

c. who the doctors said would never walk or talk, but he did.

d. showed that people can live with great pain and still die with dignity.

B. Write a sentence to introduce the example you are using.

_____

_____

_____

Using Quotations

> Quotations can be used to support an argument in a composition. Both *direct quotations,* where you give the exact words of the speaker, and *indirect quotations,* where you give the general ideas of the speaker, can be used. (See the appendix for the rules on punctuation of direct quotations.)
>
> *Examples:*   Direct quotation: He said, "I want to live, but not tied to a machine."
>
> Indirect quotation: He said (that) he wanted to live, but not tied to a machine.
>
> Remember to use the correct form of the verb in past-tense indirect quotations.

Is there a quotation you can use in your composition? Write it here.

_____

_____

Making Generalizations

> Generalizations made in English are different from those in many other languages. When English speakers talk about subjects in general, they use either the singular or plural *indefinite* form. The definite article *the* is not used.
>
> *Examples:*   We should not let *children* with brain damage die.
>
> We should not let *a child* with brain damage die.
>
> With noncount nouns, no article is used.
>
> *Example:*   Through modern *technology,* many children are kept alive.

Which of these nouns are noncount? On a separate page, write sentences using each of the nouns with a general meaning.

1. mental retardation
2. research
3. hospital
4. machine
5. life
6. baby
7. brain damage
8. doctor
9. parent
10. operation

Writing the First Draft

Write your composition. Use your introduction and example with its transition sentence. Use restrictive adjective clauses and quotations if you can. Write on every other line so you can revise your paragraph easily.

REVISING AND EDITING

Revising Your Writing

Look at the composition you wrote and check it for these elements.

1. Content

   a. Did you support your opinion with good reasons and information?
   b. Is your composition interesting?

2. Organization

   a. Do you have an introduction, supporting paragraphs, and a conclusion?
   b. Is your focus clear?
   c. Did you give examples to support your reasons?

3. Cohesion and style

   a. Did you introduce your examples with transitions?
   b. Did you use quotations to support your argument?
   c. Did you use restrictive adjective clauses to identify people, places, and things where necessary?

Editing Practice

Using *the* in Sentences with *of* + *Noun Phrase*

> The article *the* appears before specific nouns—people, places, or things that are one of a kind (*the earth*), already mentioned (*the patient in the hospital we talked about*), or members of a group (*the doctors at St. Joseph's Hospital*). It is also used before a noun followed by *of* + *noun phrase*.
>
> noun phrase
>
> *Example:*   I am against the use of life-support systems.
>
> The noun *use* is specified in this sentence by the phrase with *of* that follows it.

A. Write sentences using these nouns + phrases with *of*. Put *the* in the correct places.

1. worth of an individual's life

    _____

2. courage of the dying man

    _____

3. preservation of individual rights

    _____

B. Here are the first paragraphs of the composition on page 146. Edit them and rewrite them correctly. Check the use of indefinite forms when marking generalizations. Also, check for the use of *the* in sentences with *of* + *noun phrase*. Then compare it with the composition on page 146.

People on life-support machines are all different and in different situations. For that and other reasons, I believe family and doctor of patient on a life-support machine should be able to decide whether to remove the person from the machine or not. If the person on the machine is able to participate in decision, he or she should definitely have the right to choose.

With a modern technology, it is very difficult to determine what is real life and what is artificial life. Is a person who is breathing with help of a machine but whose brain is dead really alive or not? No one can say for sure because each individual situation is different.

I recently saw a program on T.V. that illustrates how the government's interference causes the great suffering. A machine was breathing for a man who was dying of cancer and he wanted to be removed from it. He said, "I want to live, but not tied to machine." When he tried to turn off the machine himself, the doctors tied his hands to the bed because they thought the government would sue them if man died. I think it is wrong to ignore the patient's wishes.

Editing Your Writing

Edit the composition you wrote. You can also give it to a partner. Use this checklist.

GRAMMAR

1. Indefinite forms
2. Use the *the* in sentences with *of + noun phrase*

FORM

1. Essay form: introduction, three supporting paragraphs, conclusion
2. Indentation, margins, capitalization
3. Punctuation of quotations, if any
4. Spelling

Writing the Second Draft

After you edit your composition, rewrite it neatly, using good handwriting and correct form.

PART FOUR

COMMUNICATING THROUGH WRITING

Sharing

Give your composition to your teacher for comments.

Have a debate on the question you wrote about. The class will divide into two teams, with one team taking the affirmative and one the negative side.

First meet with the members of your team and read each others' compositions. Make a list of your arguments. Then try to guess what the other team will argue and think of reasons against their arguments (rebuttals).

Choose three students to represent each side. One will give the arguments (about five minutes), one the rebuttal (about three minutes), and one the summary (about three minutes).

Using Feedback

Look at your teacher's comments. If you don't understand something, ask about it. Answer these questions.

1. What have you learned in the course so far?

    _____

    _____

    _____

    _____

2. Is there anything else you would like to study in the course?

    _____

    _____

Developing Your Skills

A. Find a persuasive article in the editorial section of your local newspaper. With a partner, outline the article. How many paragraphs does it have? Is there an introductory paragraph? How many reasons for his or her opinion does the author present? What examples does the author use? Are you persuaded by his or her argument? Why or why not?

B. Write a three-paragraph essay taking the *opposite* side of the question you wrote about for this chapter. You may get opposite points of view by recalling what the other side said during the debate you held or by interviewing a classmate who disagrees with you.

Developing Fluency

A. Write for fifteen minutes on a person who has overcome a great handicap. It can be someone you know or a famous person.

B. Write in your journal on any topic that you want to.

11

THE MEDIA

GETTING READY TO WRITE

Exploring Ideas

Discussing a News Event

A. Look at the pictures of a flood and an accident. Discuss what information you would expect to find in an article about each event.

B. Write five questions you would expect each article to answer.

THE FLOOD

1. _____

2. _____

3. _____

4. _____

5. _____

154

© STEVE SKLOOT/PHOTO RESEARCHERS

© JAN LUKAS/PHOTO RESEARCHERS

THE ACCIDENT

1. _____
2. _____
3. _____
4. _____
5. _____

C. In this chapter you are going to write a short article about a fire. Write five questions you would expect an article to answer about the fire in the picture below.

1. _____

2. _____

3. _____

4. _____

5. _____

© CHARLES HARBUTT/ARCHIVE

Building Vocabulary

Add to this list any new vocabulary or expressions from your discussion and questions.

Nouns	Verbs	Adjectives	Other
blaze	break out	burned	overcome by
fire company	injure	burning	smoke
firefighters	rescue	heroic	
firetruck	save	hospitalized	_____
flames	trap	injured	
hero, heroine			
(the) injured	_____	_____	_____
injury			
smoke	_____	_____	_____
victim			
	_____	_____	
_____			
_____	_____	_____	
_____			
_____			

Organizing Ideas

Answering Questions in an Article About an Event

> The first paragraph of an article gives you the most important facts. It usually answers these questions.
>
> Who?   What?   Where?   When?   Why?

A. Read the following article. Then underline the words that answer the questions above.

Man and Two Boys Missing Off Cape Cod

A 65-year-old man, his ten-year-old grandson, and another boy were missing yesterday after their empty boat was found off Cape Cod, the Coast Guard said. Police and Coast Guard units, which included two helicopters and four boats, searched through the night for the missing man and boys. The missing were Joseph Miller, a retired teacher, his grandson Eric Miller, and Eric's friend Anthony Blondell, 9, all from Northport, Florida. Anthony's father, John Blondell, said that Mr. Miller took the boys fishing with

© PETER VANDERMARK/STOCK, BOSTON

A Coast Guard search unit

him on Friday morning. When the three did not return home by dark, Miller's daughter-in-law called the police. Miller's empty boat was found at about 11:00 A.M. yesterday, approximately one mile from Cape Cod. Coast Guard investigators say they have no idea what happened to the three.

"All Joe wanted to do was go fishing," said Rick Mendoza, 48, a close friend of Miller's and the last one to see the man and the boys alive.

B. Imagine that there has been a fire somewhere at your school. Record information about this imaginary fire for your article. Answer these questions:

1. Who? _____

_____

2. What? _____

_____

3. Where? _____

_____

4. When? _____

_____

5. Why? _____

_____

Adding a Title

The titles of stories for newspapers and magazines must get the readers' attention in as few words as possible. Therefore the verb *be* and articles are often omitted.

Fact: A man was killed by a hit and run driver.

Title: Man Killed by Hit and Run Driver

Fact: A hurricane is approaching the East Coast.

Title: Hurricane Approaching East Coast

Fact: First National Bank was robbed by a man in a Santa Claus suit.

Title: First National Bank Robbed by Man in Santa Claus Suit

A. Rewrite these sentences as titles; omit any unnecessary words.

1. A provincial capital was taken over by guerrillas.

   _____

2. The Waldorf Art Museum was destroyed by an explosion.

   _____

3. Four people were killed in a plane crash.

   _____

4. Killer bees are threatening cattle in Texas.

   _____

5. A convicted murderer was executed.

   _____

B. Write a title for your article. _____

PART TWO

DEVELOPING WRITING SKILLS

Developing Cohesion and Style

Using Adjective Clauses

Read this paragraph.

> There was a fire in Middletown yesterday. It started in a warehouse and quickly spread to three nearby stores. The fire burned for four hours. The fire did $100,000 worth of damage. The fire killed one security guard and injured another.

The paragraph would sound much better if its five short sentences were combined into two longer sentences.

> A fire that started in a Middletown warehouse yesterday and quickly spread to three nearby stores did $100,000 worth of damage. The fire, which burned for four hours, killed one security guard and injured another.

Note that the combined sentences contain two different kinds of adjective clauses. The adjective clause in the first sentence does not have commas before and after it. This type of clause is called a *restrictive adjective clause*. It contains information that is essential to the sentence and identifies the noun modified by answering the question *"which one?"*

The second type of adjective clause is called a *nonrestrictive adjective clause*. The information in a nonrestrictive adjective clause is not essential to the sentence; it is set off by commas.

Using Restrictive Adjective Clauses: Review

Combine the information in these sentences, using restrictive relative clauses.

1. A seventeen-year-old girl is in critical condition at Long Island Hospital. She was hit by a car last night.

   _____

   _____

2. A volcano erupted on the island of Hawaii yesterday. It has destroyed ten homes.

_____

_____

3. Three children escaped without injury from their burning home. They were playing with matches.

_____

_____

4. The miners' strike will be settled soon. It has paralyzed Britain's coal industry.

_____

_____

5. A policeman wounded a robber. The robber was trying to steal an elderly woman's purse.

_____

_____

Using Nonrestrictive Adjective Clauses

A. Combine the information in these sentences, using nonrestrictive adjective clauses beginning with *who, which, whose, where,* or *when.* Remember to set off the clause with commas. (For information on punctuating adjective clauses, see the appendix.)

1. Tracy O'Brian was crossing Wantaugh Avenue. She was a senior at Wantaugh High School.

_____

_____

2. The volcano has erupted several times in recent years. It is one of the most active volcanoes in the world.

_____

_____

3. The children were rescued by a neighbor. The children's mother was at the store.

_____

_____

4. Brian McDonald said that he believes the miners will go back to work next week. Brian McDonald is the head of the Miners' Union.

   _____

   _____

5. The old woman was taken to Fairfield Hospital. The elderly woman had tried to fight off her attacker.

   _____

   _____

6. On Christmas Day two gunmen tried to rob a bank. On this day, most people are at home with their families.

   _____

   _____

7. In Thailand two tourists were arrested for sitting on the head of a statue of Buddha. In Thailand most people are Buddhists.

   _____

   _____

B. Rewrite this paragraph on a separate page. Combine the sentences within parentheses, using restrictive and nonrestrictive adjective clauses.

(A tugboat disappeared off the Connecticut coast yesterday. The tugboat carried six crew members.) (The boat left Bridgeport harbor at 8:00 P.M. on Saturday. The tugboat was on its way out to sea.) (A helicopter was sent in search of the tugboat. The tugboat was supposed to arrive on Saturday night.) (The president of the tugboat company said that they will not stop searching until the tugboat is found. The president's son is aboard the tugboat.)

C. Look at the information you wrote for your paragraph. Write three sentences using restrictive and/or nonrestrictive adjective clauses.

   _____

   _____

   _____

   _____

   _____

   _____

Using Reduced Clauses

Good writers generally try to use as few words as possible. Therefore, they often leave out unnecessary words in adjective clauses. Here are two ways to do this:

1. You can omit the relative pronoun if it refers to the *object* of a restrictive adjective clause.

    Example: The man *that* the policeman caught was wearing a Santa Claus suit. →
    The man the policeman caught was wearing a Santa Claus suit.

2. You can omit the pronoun and the auxiliary verb *be* in restrictive and nonrestrictive adjective clauses.

    Examples: First National Bank, *which is* protected by Benson Security, was robbed yesterday. →
    First National Bank, protected by Benson Security, was robbed yesterday.

    The girl *who was* missing for two days was found unharmed. →
    The girl missing for two days was found unharmed.

    Several firefighters *who were* on the scene were overcome by smoke. →
    Several firefighters on the scene were overcome by smoke.

You can also use present participles in reduced adverbial clauses.

Examples: She was injured *while she was* trying to put our the fire. →
She was injured trying to put out the fire.

When she opened the safe, she found her jewelry gone. →
Opening the safe, she found her jewelry gone.

© ABRAHAM MENASHE/PHOTO RESEARCHERS

A. Read this paragraph and omit any unnecessary words.

Fire in Cameron Hotel

A two-alarm fire broke out on the sixth floor of the beautiful and expensive Cameron Hotel early yesterday. The fire, which was controlled by firefighters after four hours, caused extensive damage to the hotel, although no serious injuries were reported. The blaze started in a resident's room of the twelve-story hotel at 222 W. 23rd Street shortly after 3:00 A.M. Someone said that the blaze was caused by a guest who was smoking in bed. While they struggled to control the flames, four firefighters were overcome by smoke and taken to Roosevelt Hospital. Fire officials who were on the scene said that there will be an official investigation into the cause of the fire.

B. Look at the sentences you wrote for your article. Are there any words that can be omitted?

Writing the First Draft

Write your article using the notes you made in Part One. Use adjective clauses and be careful to omit unnecessary words. Write on every other line so you can revise your paragraph easily.

PART THREE

REVISING AND EDITING

Revising Your Writing

Distinguishing Fact from Opinion

> When a reporter writes an article about an event, he or she usually gives only facts. It is not appropriate for reporters to give their personal opinions or to include information that may or may not be correct.

A. Read this paragraph. Draw a line through any information that should not be included—information that is the reporter's opinion and not fact.

Fumes from Chemical Plant Send Dozens to Hospital

A cloud of sulfuric acid fumes sickened thirty-six people as it swept across downtown Middleport yesterday. The poisonous cloud came from the Kozar Chemical Plant in Santa Clara, California, which should be closed. Officials at the plant say that the sulfuric acid escaped as it was being transferred from one tank to another. I think this was very careless of the plant workers. Two weeks ago there was a similar accident at this plant. Most people believe that the plant officials should be fired for their carelessness.

B. Look at your article carefully. Check it for these elements:

1. Content
    a. Is there any information you should omit because it is not factual?
    b. Will your title capture the interest of the readers?

2. Organization

    Did you answer the questions "who?" "what?" "where?" "when?" and "why?"

3. Cohesion and style
    a. Did you use adjective clauses to combine information?
    b. Did you omit unnecessary words and use reduced clauses where possible?

Editing Practice

Using Commas with Nonrestrictive Clauses

Edit this article for the use of commas with nonrestrictive clauses.

Janet Reese a ten-year-old burn victim who was set on fire by her mother two years ago wants to help other child-abuse victims around the country. She is being treated at the Miami Burn Center and says that other children, who have gone through similar experiences, can get encouragement from her experience.

Specialists at the Burn Center a team of doctors and nurses who are among the best in the country are impressed by her courage and determination. The doctor, who is treating her, said that her courage and will to live were the things that really kept her alive.

Janet is sending letters to other burn patients, who are victims of child abuse. She tells them that she was hurt, but she got better, and they can too.

Editing Your Writing

Edit the article you wrote. You can also give it to a partner to check. Use this checklist.

GRAMMAR

Adjective clauses

FORM

1. Paragraph form: indentation, margins, capitalization
2. Punctuation of nonrestrictive adjective clauses
3. Spelling

Writing the Second Draft

After you edit your article, rewrite it neatly, using good handwriting and correct form.

PART FOUR

COMMUNICATING THROUGH WRITING

Sharing

Give your article to your teacher for comments.

The class can make a school newspaper. Choose some of the articles about the fire. Also write some other articles about anything interesting that has happened to the students at the school. You can write about accidents, important events, sports, family life, or achievements.

Using Feedback

Look at your teacher's comments. If you don't understand something, ask about it. Look at the other papers you have written. Do you have problems with subject-verb or pronoun agreement? Correct any mistakes in agreement. When you edit other papers in the future, make sure you pay special attention to agreement of verbs and pronouns.

Developing Your Skills

Find an article in a newspaper or a magazine on a subject that interests you. Try to find one that has three or more paragraphs. Read the article carefully. Then, without looking at it, summarize the information in the article in *one* sentence. (*Hint:* Answer as many of the *wh-* questions—"Who?" "What?" etc.—as you can in one well-written sentence.) Then expand your one-sentence summary to *one* paragraph. Exchange your work with a classmate. Give him or her the sentence to read first, then the paragraph, and, finally, the original article.

Developing Fluency

A. Write for fifteen minutes on the most frightening experience you have ever had. Then write for fifteen minutes on the saddest experience you have ever had. Finally, write for fifteen minutes on the happiest experience you have ever had.

B. With a partner, discuss the writing assignments for A above. Which was the easiest to write? Why? Which was the most difficult? Why? For which experience could you remember the most details? Why?

12

PREJUDICE, TOLERANCE, AND JUSTICE

GETTING READY TO WRITE

Exploring Ideas

Discussing Community Problems

A. Look at the pictures on the next page. Each one shows a solution to a problem. What problem is represented by each picture?

B. List on the board problems that people in your community or school have. Then choose a problem you are interested in and discuss possible solutions in small groups. Try to think of as many solutions as you can.

C. Write a proposal to solve the problem you choose. Use *should* or *shouldn't* in your proposal.

_____

_____

_____

_____

_____

A new day-care center for the students and staff of a local community college

New low-cost housing for city residents

A cafeteria whose menu has been changed to include foods its international students have requested

More and more international students are remaining in the United States and becoming citizens.

D. Write two to four reasons why you think that your proposal is a good one.

1. _____

2. _____

3. _____

4. _____

Building Vocabulary

Add new vocabulary from your discussion to this list.

Nouns	Verbs	Adjectives	Other
advantage	benefit	beneficial	
benefit	establish	expensive	_____
disadvantage	give ____ a		
establishment	chance	_____	_____
expense	improve		
improvement	organize	_____	_____
organization	raise objections		
		_____	_____
_____	_____		
		_____	_____
_____	_____		
		_____	_____
_____	_____		
		_____	
_____			

Organizing Ideas

Determining Who Your Audience Is

In this chapter you are going to write a persuasive essay. In your essay, you will try to convince a group of people that your proposal is a good one. The arguments that you use will depend on who your audience is. For example, if you think that the classes in your school should be limited to twelve students, you will have to try to convince the school administration. If you think that students who speak a language other than English in the classroom should be fined, you will have to convince your classmates and your teacher.

Who is the audience for your essay?

_____

Countering Objections to Your Proposal

Once you know who your audience is, you will have to try to think of some objections that they may have to your proposal. You have to imagine what their viewpoint is. For example, in answer to a proposal that classes in your school should be limited to twelve students, the school administrators might have these two objections:

1. There is no money to hire more teachers.
2. There are not enough classrooms to divide the classes.

To convince them that classes should be smaller, you will have to counter these objections. The best way to do this is to provide possible solutions to the objections.

1. Can you think of any possible solutions to the first objection?
2. Can you think of any possible solutions to the second objection?

A. Look at this proposal:

Students who speak their native language in the classroom should be fined 25 cents.

B. List two possible objections to this proposal.

1. _____
2. _____

C. List counterarguments to these objections.

1. _____
2. _____

D. List some objections that your audience might have to your proposal.

1. _____
2. _____
3. _____
4. _____

E. List possible counterarguments to these objections.

1. _____
2. _____
3. _____
4. _____

Making an Outline

Your composition will include an introductory paragraph and a closing paragraph. In addition, there will be one paragraph for each of your arguments and a paragraph listing possible objections and countering them. It is often easier to organize this type of writing by putting it in a simplified outline form:

I.   Introductory paragraph: states proposal and lists arguments for it
II.   Persuasive argument 1: develops the first argument and says why your proposal should be carried out
III. Persuasive argument 2: develops the second argument
IV.   Counterarguments: counters objections
V.   Concluding paragraph: summarizes reasons for the solution you proposed

Here is a sample outline.

I.   Introductory paragraph
    1. ABC English Language Academy should start a cooperative day-care center.
    2. It would benefit both the community and the school.

II.   Argument 1
    1. It would benefit the community:
       a. Mothers of young children cannot attend English classes because they cannot afford to hire babysitters.
       b. Many women have no chance to learn English and feel uncomfortable living in the United States.
       c. Their children do not learn English until they go to school.
       d. Mothers cannot help children with their schoolwork because of the language barrier.

© BARBARA RIOS/PHOTO RESEARCHERS

III. Argument 2
    1. It would benefit the school:
        a. People would feel that the school was really interested in helping the community (public relations).
        b. Staff members could have good day care for their children.
        c. It would help attract a better staff.
        d. It would make the staff feel more content.
        e. School enrollment would increase.

IV. Counterarguments
    1. To the objection that it would be difficult for the school to organize:
        a. A student-staff organizing committee could be created.
        b. Several interested students and staff members have experience working in day-care centers.
        c. The committee would take complete responsibility for obtaining licenses and other such tasks.
    2. To the objection that it would cost the school too much money:
        a. Because it would be a cooperative, students and staff would volunteer their time.
        b. Participating students and staff members could bring in used toys, books, etc.
        c. A small enrollment fee could be used to cover the cost of furniture and other necessary items.
        d. There is a possibility that the government would help fund the center.

V. Concluding paragraph

Now make a similar outline for your essay. Your essay may have from four to six paragraphs. Just remember that each separate argument should be stated in a new paragraph.

PART TWO

DEVELOPING WRITING SKILLS
Developing Cohesion and Style
Using the Conditional Mood

Do these sentences refer to conditions that presently exist or to conditions that might or could exist *if* something else were true?

1. If I were rich, I *would* buy a Mercedes Benz.
2. If you paid attention in class, you *could* learn to speak English.
3. If Ricardo tried jogging, he *might* lose weight.

In your essay, you will probably have to use the auxiliaries *would, could,* and *might* because your arguments, objections, and counterarguments will be based on the condition that your proposal is accepted. For example, suppose that your proposal is:

Class size should be limited to twelve students.

The condition "if class size were limited to twelve students" will be the basis of your entire composition, even if it is not written with each sentence.

Example: (if class size were limited to twelve students) The teachers *would* be able to spend more time with each student. In addition, (if the class size were limited to twelve students) the students *might* get to know each other better. Finally, (if the class size were limited to twelve students) students *could* practice speaking more.

Read the following paragraph. Complete it by circling the correct auxiliaries. Remember to use *would, could,* or *might* when there is a condition that is not presently true or real.

I believe that students in our class should be fined for speaking their native language during class time. This (*will/would*)₁ have several benefits. First of all, students (*will/would*)₂ learn to rely on English more. Second, students who don't speak the same native language (*might/can*)₃ get to know each other better. Third, students (*will/would*)₄ be more likely to tell the teacher when they are having problems. Finally, we (*can/could*)₅ use the money from the fines to have a party at the end of the semester.

Using Linking Expressions and Transition Words for Enumerating Ideas

Most of your essay will consist of lists. There will be a list of arguments in favor of your proposal, a list of possible objections, and a list of counterarguments to the objections. Since there are so many places where you will have to list or enumerate ideas, it is important to try to use several different linking expressions and transition words. You can use these expressions at the beginning of each new paragraph and within the paragraphs themselves.

Here are some of the most common ways to add ideas to a composition.

	Example	
First Idea	A day-care center would benefit the community by making it possible for mothers of young children to attend class.	
	Linking Expressions	**Examples**
Additional Ideas	also	It would *also* benefit the school . . . *Another benefit* would be that . . .
	at the same time besides + noun *or* noun phrase	*At the same time,* teachers would benefit. *Besides* benefiting the community, it would benefit the school. (*Besides* this, it would benefit the school.)
	furthermore	*Furthermore,* the school would benefit.
	in addition	*In addition,* the school would benefit
	moreover	*Moreover,* the school would benefit.
	similarly	*Similarly,* it would benefit the school.

Here are some common transition words for listing ideas in order.

Transition Words	Examples
first (of all)	*First of all,* mothers of young children would be able to attend classes.
second	*Second,* school staff members would be able to use the center.
finally	*Finally,* the school would also receive many benefits from this type of program.

Complete the following paragraph with transition words and linking expressions; choose from those given in this section. Add punctuation where necessary.

There are several ways that the community would benefit from the establishment of a day-care center. _____ it would give non-English speakers a chance to go to school to learn English, and they would become more integrated into the life of the community. _____ improving community relations, a day-care center would help non-English-speaking parents raise their standard of living because, if they learned English, they could get better jobs. _____ the parents would be able to help their children with their schoolwork and communicate with their teachers. _____ a day-care center would give non-English-speaking children and English-speaking children a chance to get to know each other. _____ all parents (not just non-English speakers) would have a place to leave their children while they work.

Using Connecting Words and Transitions for Contrasting Ideas and Showing Cause and Result: Review

In your second-to-last paragraph, you will list possible objections and then counter them. To do this, you will need to review some of the connecting words and transitions you have already learned.

CONNECTING WORDS AND TRANSITIONS FOR CONTRASTING IDEAS

although	even though	nevertheless
but	however	while

CONNECTING WORDS AND TRANSITIONS FOR SHOWING CAUSE AND RESULT

as a result	consequently	so
because	since	therefore

Complete the following paragraph by circling the correct connecting words or transitions.

Several objections to a day-care center may be raised. First of all, some people may say that it is impossible (*because/although*)₁ it would be difficult to organize. (*However/Therefore*),₂ there are several students and staff members who have day-care experience and are willing to set it up. Another objection might be that it would be expensive (*while/so*)₃ the school would have to raise tuition. (*Consequently/But*)₄ this is not necessarily true. (*Since/Although*)₅ there would be some initial expense, it can be kept to a minimum by having participants donate used toys and books and pay a small enrollment fee.

Writing a Concluding Paragraph

Read this concluding paragraph and then answer the following questions about it.

In conclusion, because of the benefits to both the school and the community, the advantages of a day-care center clearly outweigh the disadvantages; therefore, I hope that the school administration will consider this proposal carefully.

1. What transition expression does the paragraph begin with? Other possible concluding expressions are *in summary* and *to conclude*.
2. Did the writer restate the ideas in different words?
3. How did the writer end the concluding paragraph? Did the writer use *will* or *would* with the hope?

Writing the First Draft

Write your essay using the outline you made. Remember to use transitions and connecting words in the essay. Write on every other line so you can revise your paragraphs easily.

PART THREE

REVISING AND EDITING

Revising Your Writing

With the help of a partner, read and revise your essay. Check your essay for these elements.

1. Content

   a. Did you state your proposal clearly?
   b. Did you give good reasons to support your proposal?

2. Organization

   a. Did you begin with an introductory paragraph and end with a concluding paragraph?
   b. Did you write at least two paragraphs developing your arguments?
   c. Did you give good counterarguments in one paragraph?

3. Cohesion and style

   a. Did you use transition words when listing your ideas?
   b. Did you use connecting words and transitions when showing cause, result, and contrast?
   c. Did you use the conditional mood in the appropriate places?

Editing Practice

Edit this paragraph for all errors, and rewrite it correctly. Then check it against the paragraph on page 176.

There is several way that the community would beneficial from establishment of day-care center. First, it would give non-English speakers a chance to go to school to learn English, and they will become more integrated into the life of the community. Besides improve community relations, a day-care center will help non-English-speaking parents raise their standard of living because, if they learned English, they can get better jobs. Also, parent would be able to help their children with their schoolwork and communicate with their teachers. Moreover, a day-care center gives non-English-speaking children and English-speaking children a chance to get to know one another. Finally, all parents (not just non-English speakers) would have a place to leave its child while they work.

Editing Your Writing

Edit the essay you wrote. You can also give it to a partner. Use this checklist.

GRAMMAR
The conditional mood

FORM
1. Essay form: Introduction, supporting paragraphs, conclusion
2. Indentation, margins, capitalization
3. Punctuation of sentences with transitions
4. Spelling

Writing the Second Draft

After you edit your essay, rewrite it neatly, using good handwriting and correct form.

PART FOUR

COMMUNICATING THROUGH WRITING

Sharing

Give your essay to your teacher for comments.

Present your essay to the class as a speech. First, write the main ideas and important phrases on notecards. Then, on your own, practice giving the speech. Speak slowly and stress important words. Pause between phrases. Get to know the speech so that you can look at the audience while you speak.

Using Feedback

Since this is the end of the course, you should now do a self-evaluation. Look at the comments your teacher has given you throughout the course and answer these questions.

1. How have you improved?
2. What are your strong points?
3. What are your weak points?
4. What should you be especially careful of when you revise?
5. What should you be especially careful of when you edit?
6. How do you feel about writing in English now?

Developing Your Skills

A. Look at the paragraph on page 174 on fining students for speaking their native language during class time. You are going to expand this paragraph into a six-paragraph essay. Work in small groups. Begin by outlining the four arguments the author presents. Then suggest details and examples to further develop each of the four arguments. Finally, write out the new essay, including introductory and concluding paragraphs.

B. Working on your own, write a four- to six-paragraph essay taking the opposite side of the English-only issue presented in the preceding activity. (Or take the opposite side of your own essay that you wrote for this chapter.)

C. Find articles in newspapers and magazines on the "English-Only" movement in the United States. (Use the *Readers' Guide to Periodical Literature* in the library to find the articles. Look under the heading of "English Only"—the librarian will help you.) Bring copies of these articles to class and discuss them with your classmates. What are some of the arguments of the proponents (the people who are *for* the issue)? What are the opposing viewpoints? What is your opinion?

Developing Fluency

A. Write for fifteen minutes on the most important issue or problem facing you in your life at this moment.

B. Write (for as long as you wish) on a possible solution to the problem or issue you described in the preceding activity.

APPENDICES

APPENDIX 1

Spelling Rules for Adding Endings

Rules for Adding Endings that Begin with Vowels (-*ed*, -*ing*, -*er*, -*est*)

1. For words ending in a silent *e*, drop the *e* and add the ending.

   like → lik**ed**   make → mak**ing**   safe → saf**er**   fine → fin**est**

2. For one-syllable words ending in a single vowel and a single consonant, double the final consonant.

   bat → bat**ted**   run → run**ning**   fat → fat**ter**   hot → hot**test**

3. Don't double the final consonant when the word has two final consonants or two vowels before a final consonant.

   pick → pick**ed**   sing → sing**ing**   clean → clean**er**   cool → cool**est**

4. For words of two or more syllables that end in a single vowel and a single consonant, double the final consonant if the word is accented on the final syllable.

   refer′ → refer**red**   impel′ → impel**led**

5. For words of two or more syllables that end in a single vowel and single consonant, make no change if the word isn't accented on the final syllable.

   tra′vel → travel**ed**   fo′cus → focus**ed**

6. For words ending in a consonant and *y*, change the *y* to *i* and add the ending *unless the ending begins with* i.

  study → stud**ied**   dirty → dirt**ier**   sunny → sunn**iest**
  study → study**ing**   hurry → hurry**ing**

7. For words ending in a vowel and *y*, make no change before adding the ending.

  play → play**ed**   stay → stay**ing**

Rules for Adding Endings that Begin with Consonants (*-ly, -ment*)

8. For words ending in a silent *e*, make no change when adding endings that begin with consonants.

  fine → fine**ly**   state → state**ment**

9. For words ending in a consonant and *y*, change the *y* to *i* before adding the ending.

  happy → happ**ily**   merry → merr**iment**

Rules for Adding a Final *s* to Nouns and Verbs

10. Generally, add the *s* without making changes.

  sit → sits   dance → dances   play → plays   book → books

11. If a word ends in a consonant and *y*, change the *y* to *i* and add *es*.

  marry → marr**ies**   study → stud**ies**   cherry → cherr**ies**

12. If a word ends in *ch, s, sh, x,* or *z*, add *es:*

  church → church**es**   boss → boss**es**   mix → mix**es**
  cash → cash**es**   fizz → fizz**es**

13. For words ending in *o*, sometimes add *es* and sometimes add *s:*

  tomato → tomato**es**   potato → potato**es**
  piano → pianos   radio → radios

14. For words ending in *f* or *fe,* generally drop the *f* for *fe* and add *ves:*

  knife → kni**ves**   wife → wi**ves**   life → li**ves**   loaf → loa**ves**

  Exceptions: safe → safes   puff → puffs   roof → roofs

APPENDIX 2

Capitalization Rules

First Words

1. Capitalize the first word of every sentence.

    They live in Rome.   **Who** is it?

2. Capitalize the first word of a quotation.

    He said, "**My** name is Paul."   Jenny asked, "**When** is the party?"

Personal Names

3. Capitalize names of people, including initials and titles of address.

    Mrs. Jones   **Mohandas Gandhi**   **John F. Kennedy**

4. Capitalize family words if used alone or followed by a name.

    Let's go, **Dad**.   Where's **Grandma**?   She's at **Aunt Lucy's**.

5. Don't capitalize family words if used with a possessive pronoun or article.

    my **uncle**   her **mother**   our **grandparents**   an **aunt**

6. Capitalize the pronoun *I*.

    I have a book.   She's bigger than **I** am.

7. Capitalize names of God.

    God   **Allah**   **Jesus Christ**

8. Capitalize the names of nationalities, races, peoples, and religions.

    Arab   **Asian**   **Chicano**   **Muslim**

9. Generally, don't capitalize occupations.

    I am a **secretary**.   She wants to be a **lawyer**.

Place Names

10. Capitalize the names of countries, states, provinces, and cities.

    Mexico   **New York**   **Ontario**   **Tokyo**

11. Capitalize the names of oceans, lakes, rivers, islands, and mountains.

    the Atlantic Ocean   **Lake Como**   **the Amazon**
    Mt. Everest   **Belle Isle**

12. Capitalize the names of geographical areas.

    the South   **the East Coast**   **Asia**   **Antarctica**

13. Don't capitalize directions if they aren't names of geographical areas.

> He lives **e**ast of Toronto.   They traveled **s**outhwest.

14. Capitalize names of schools, parks, buildings, and streets.

> the University of Georgia   Central Park
> the Sears Building   Oxford Road

Time Words

15. Capitalize names of days and months.

> Monday   Friday   January   March

16. Capitalize names of holidays and historical events.

> Christmas   New Year's Day   Independence Day   World War II

17. Don't capitalize names of seasons.

> spring   summer   fall   winter

Titles

18. Capitalize the first word and all important words of titles of books, magazines, newspapers, and articles.

> *Interactions*   *Newsweek*   *The New York Times*   "Rock Music Today"

19. Capitalize the first word and all important words of names of movies, plays, radio programs, and television programs.

> *The African Queen*   *The Tempest*   "News Roundup"   "Fame"

20. Don't capitalize articles (*a, an, the*), conjunctions (*but, and, or*), and short prepositions (*of, with, in, on, for*) unless they are the first word of a title.

> *The Life of Thomas Edison*   *War and Peace*   *Death of a Salesman*

Names of Organizations

21. Capitalize the names of organizations, government groups, and businesses.

> International Student Association   the Senate   Gestetner

22. Capitalize trade names, but do not capitalize the name of the product.

> **IBM** typewriter   **Toyota** hatchback   **Kellogg's** cereal

Other

23. Capitalize the names of languages.

> Spanish   Thai   French   Japanese

24. Don't capitalize school subjects unless they are the names of languages or are followed by a number.

> geometry   music   English   Arabic   Biology 306

APPENDIX 3

Punctuation Rules

Period

1. Use a period after a statement or command.

    We are studying English.   Open your books to Chapter 3.

2. Use a period after most abbreviations.

    Mr.   Ms.   Dr.   Ave.   etc.   U.S.

    Exceptions: UN   NATO   IBM   AIDS

3. Use a period after initials.

    H. G. Wells   Dr. H. R. Hammond

Question Mark

4. Use a question mark after (not before) questions.

    Where are you going?   Is he here yet?

5. In a direct quotation, the question mark goes before the quotation marks.

    He asked, "What's your name?"

Exclamation Point

6. Use an exclamation point after exclamatory sentences or phrases.

    I won the lottery!   Be quiet!   Wow!

Comma

7. Use a comma before a conjunction (*and, or, so, but*) that separates two independent clauses.

    She wanted to go to work, so she decided to take an English course.
    He wasn't happy in that apartment, but he didn't have the money to move.

8. Don't use a comma before a conjunction that separates two phrases that aren't complete sentences.

    She worked in the library and studied at night.
    Do you want to go to a movie or stay home?

9. Use a comma after an introductory clause or phrase (generally if it is five or more words long)

    After a beautiful wedding ceremony, they had a reception in her mother's home.
    If you want to write well, you should practice writing almost every night.

10. Use a comma to separate interrupting expressions from the rest of a sentence.

> Do you know, by the way, what time dinner is?
> Many of the students, I found out, stayed on campus during the summer.

11. Use a comma after transitional expressions.

> In addition, he stole all her jewelry.
> However, he left the T.V.

Common transitional expressions are:

therefore	moreover	however
consequently	furthermore	nevertheless
for this reason	besides	on the other hand
also	in fact	for example
in addition	similarly	for instance

12. Use a comma to separate names of people in direct address from the rest of a sentence.

> Jane, have you seen Paul?
> We aren't sure, Mrs. Shapiro, where he is.

13. Use a comma after *yes* and *no* in answers.

> Yes, he was here a minute ago.
> No, I haven't.

14. Use a comma to separate items in a series.

> We have coffee, tea, and milk.
> He looked in the refrigerator, on the shelves, and in the cupboard.

15. Use a comma to separate an appositive from the rest of a sentence.

> Mrs. Sampson, his English teacher, gave him a good recommendation.
> Would you like to try a taco, a delicious Mexican food?

16. If a date or address has two or more parts, use a comma after each part.

> I was born on June 5, 1968.
> The house at 230 Seventh Street, Miami, Florida, is for sale.

17. Use a comma to separate contrasting information from the rest of a sentence.

> It wasn't Maria, but Parvin, who was absent.
> Bring your writing book, not your reading book.

18. Use a comma to separate quotations from the rest of a sentence.

> He asked, "What are we going to do?"
> "I'm working downtown," he said.

19. Use a comma to separate two or more adjectives that each modify the noun alone.

> She was an intelligent, beautiful actress. (*Intelligent* and *beautiful* both modify *actress*.)
> Eat those delicious green beans. (*Delicious* modifies *green beans*.)

20. Use a comma to separate nonrestrictive clauses from the rest of a sentence. A clause is nonrestrictive if it isn't necessary to identify the noun modified. Clauses are usually nonrestrictive after:

a. proper names

> Michael Jackson, who is now touring the country, is a famous rock star.

b. nouns that have already been identified

> Tanya and Bertha Green were rescued from the fire. The girls, who are being treated at Midland Hospital, were badly injured.

c. nouns that can be identified because there is only one

> The earth, which is the fifth largest planet, has one satellite.

21. Don't use commas after restrictive clauses. A restrictive clause is needed to identify the noun modified.

> The fireman who rescued the two girls was given a medal.

Quotation Marks

22. Use quotation marks at the beginning and end of exact quotations. Other punctuation marks go before the end quotation marks.

> He said, "I'm going to Montreal."
> "How are you?" he asked.

23. Use quotation marks before and after titles of stories, articles, songs, and television programs. Periods and commas go before the final quotation marks, while question marks and exclamation points normally go after them.

> Do you like to watch "Dallas" on television?
> My favorite song is "Let It Be."
> Do you like the story "Gift of the Magi"?

Apostrophe

24. Use apostrophes in contractions.

> don't   it's   we've   they're

25. Use an apostrophe to make possessive nouns.

> *Singular:* Jerry's   my boss's
> *Plural:* the children's   the Smiths'

Underlining

26. Underline the titles of books, magazines, newspapers, plays, and movies.

> I am reading <u>One Hundred Years of Solitude</u>.
> Did you like the movie <u>It's a Wonderful Life</u>?

APPENDIX 4

A List of Noncount Nouns

Food

bread, butter, cheese, chicken,* chocolate,* coffee,* cream, fish,* flour, fruit,* ice cream,* juice,* meat, milk,* rice, salt, spaghetti, sugar, tea

Natural Phenomena

Weather words: rain, snow,* sunshine, thunder, wind*
Gases: air, hydrogen, nitrogen, oxygen
Minerals: copper, gold, iron, silver, steel
Materials: dirt, dust, earth, grass, ice, land,* oil, sand, water*

Activities and Sports

baseball,* chess, dance,* skating, soccer, tennis

Emotions and Qualities[†]

ambition, anger, courage, fear, freedom, happiness, hatred, honesty, justice, loneliness, love, joy, pride

Social Issues[†]

abortion, crime, democracy, divorce, hunger, nuclear power, peace, pollution, poverty

Mass Nouns (Composed of Dissimilar Items)

change, clothing, fruit, equipment, furniture, jewelry, luggage, mail, machinery, make-up, medicine, money, noise, scenery, technology, transportation, vocabulary

---

* These nouns are sometimes count and sometimes noncount. They are noncount when they refer to the item in general. They are count when they refer to a particular item.

> I like coffee and tea.
> Please give me one coffee and two teas.

[†] Most emotions, qualities, and social issues can function as count nouns: *a strong ambition, a deep hatred, a terrible crime.*

Subjects

art,* economics, history,* humanities, physics

Miscellaneous

advice, business,* fun, glass,* help,* homework, knowledge,* information, insurance, life, nature,* news, paint,* paper,* publicity, reality,* research, sleep, time,* traffic, trouble, tuition, work*

APPENDIX 5

Subordinating Conjunctions

Subordinating conjunctions can show relationships of *time, reason, contrast,* and *purpose.*

1. Time: when, whenever, if
2. Reason: because, since
3. Contrast: although, even though, though
4. Purpose: so that

APPENDIX 6

Transitions

Transitions are words or phrases that join two related ideas. Here is a list of the most common transitions.

1. Giving examples: for example, for instance
2. Adding emphasis: in fact, of course
3. Adding information: in addition, furthermore, moreover, besides
4. Making comparisons: similarly, likewise
5. Showing contrast: however, nevertheless, in contrast, on the contrary, on one hand/ on the other hand
6. Giving reasons or results: therefore, as a result, as a consequence, for this (that) reason
7. Giving sequences: now, then, first (second, etc.), earlier, later, meanwhile, finally

CHAPTER 1 FEEDBACK SHEET

Student Name _____ Date _____

Personal reaction:

_____

_____

_____

_____

_____

Chapter checklist:

	Good	Needs Work
Content		
1. Development of ideas	☐	☐
2. Reasons for opinions	☐	☐
Organization		
1. Topic sentence	☐	☐
2. Order of importance of ideas	☐	☐
Cohesion and style		
1. Use of *because, so,* and *therefore*	☐	☐
2. Use of *also* and *in addition*	☐	☐
3. Use of transition words *first of all* and *finally*	☐	☐
4. Use of adverbs of frequency and quantifiers to moderate opinions	☐	☐

Difficulties with grammar to work on:

_____

_____

_____

Difficulties with form to work on:

_____

_____

_____

CHAPTER 2 FEEDBACK SHEET

Student Name _____ Date _____

Personal reaction:

_____

_____

_____

_____

_____

Chapter checklist:

	Good	Needs Work
Content Use of words that describe the senses to give details	☐	☐
Organization 1. Topic sentence	☐	☐
2. All details develop topic sentence	☐	☐
3. Concluding sentence	☐	☐
Cohesion and style 1. Use of *since* to give reasons	☐	☐
2. Use of varied word order	☐	☐

Difficulties with grammar to work on:

_____

_____

_____

Difficulties with form to work on:

_____

_____

_____

CHAPTER 3 FEEDBACK SHEET

Student Name _____ Date _____

Personal reaction:

_____
_____
_____
_____
_____

Chapter checklist:

	Good	Needs Work
Content		
1. Clear statement of opinion	☐	☐
2. Examples of general statement	☐	☐
3. Predictions	☐	☐
4. Avoiding faulty reasoning	☐	☐
Organization		
1. Topic sentence	☐	☐
2. Concluding sentence	☐	☐
Cohesion and style		
1. Use of transitions	☐	☐
2. Use of *must, have to, should, ought to*	☐	☐
3. Moderate or strong style	☐	☐

Difficulties with grammar to work on:

_____
_____
_____

Difficulties with form to work on:

_____
_____
_____

CHAPTER 4 FEEDBACK SHEET

Student Name _____ Date _____

Personal reaction:

_____

_____

_____

_____

_____

Chapter checklist:

	Good	Needs Work
Content		
1. Description of best characteristics	☐	☐
2. Positive tone	☐	☐
Organization		
1. Limiting of topic	☐	☐
2. Unification of ideas	☐	☐
3. Positive topic sentence	☐	☐
4. New idea in each sentence	☐	☐
5. Concluding sentence	☐	☐
Cohesion and style		
1. Verb tenses	☐	☐
2. Use of demonstratives to unify a paragraph	☐	☐

Difficulties with grammar to work on:

_____

_____

_____

Difficulties with form to work on:

_____

_____

_____

CHAPTER 5 FEEDBACK SHEET

Student Name _____ Date _____

Personal reaction:

_____

_____

_____

_____

Chapter checklist:

	Good	Needs Work
Content		
1. Level of interest of anecdote	☐	☐
2. Clear relationship of lesson to anecdote	☐	☐
3. Background information	☐	☐
4. Use of interesting details	☐	☐
Organization		
1. Avoidance of unimportant details	☐	☐
2. Paragraph division	☐	☐
Cohesion and style		
Use of transitions and varied sentence patterns	☐	☐

Difficulties with grammar to work on:

_____

_____

_____

Difficulties with form to work on:

_____

_____

_____

CHAPTER 6 FEEDBACK SHEET

Student Name _____ Date _____

Personal reaction:

_____
_____
_____
_____
_____

Chapter checklist:

	Good	Needs Work
Content		
1. Accurate information	☐	☐
2. Relevant information	☐	☐
Organization		
1. Appropriate, interesting title	☐	☐
2. Effective use of paragraphs to express main ideas	☐	☐
Cohesion and style		
Transition words	☐	☐

Difficulties with grammar to work on:

_____
_____
_____

Difficulties with form to work on:

_____
_____
_____

CHAPTER 7 FEEDBACK SHEET

Student Name _____ Date _____

Personal reaction:

_____

_____

_____

_____

_____

Chapter checklist:

	Good	Needs Work
Content		
1. Level of interest of information	☐	☐
2. Omission of irrelevant information	☐	☐
Organization		
1. Paragraph division and organization according to time	☐	☐
2. Topic sentence	☐	☐
3. Concluding sentence	☐	☐
Cohesion and style		
1. Parallel gerund and infinitive constructions	☐	☐
2. Use of verbal adjectives	☐	☐
3. Use of *used to* and *would*	☐	☐

Difficulties with grammar to work on:

_____

_____

_____

Difficulties with form to work on:

_____

_____

_____

CHAPTER 8 FEEDBACK SHEET

Student Name _____ Date _____

Personal reaction:

_____

_____

_____

_____

Chapter checklist:

	Good	Needs Work
Content		
1. Level of interest of information	☐	☐
2. Accurate information	☐	☐
Organization		
1. Topic sentence	☐	☐
2. Paragraph on similarities	☐	☐
3. Paragraph on differences	☐	☐
Cohesion and style		
1. Use of *both* and *neither*	☐	☐
2. Use of *in contrast* and *on the other hand*	☐	☐
3. Use of *while*	☐	☐

Difficulties with grammar to work on:

_____

_____

Difficulties with form to work on:

_____

_____

_____

CHAPTER 9 FEEDBACK SHEET

Student Name _____ Date _____

Personal reaction:

_____

_____

_____

_____

Chapter checklist:

	Good	Needs Work
Content		
1. Accurate use of information	☐	☐
2. Interesting comparisons	☐	☐
Organization		
Order of information	☐	☐
Cohesion and style		
1. Use of passive voice	☐	☐
2. Varied sentence structure	☐	☐
3. Use of *with, unlike,* or *because of* + noun phrase	☐	☐
4. Use of *because* + noun	☐	☐

Difficulties with grammar to work on:

_____

_____

_____

Difficulties with form to work on:

_____

_____

_____

CHAPTER 10 FEEDBACK SHEET

Student Name _____ Date _____

Personal reaction:

_____

_____

_____

_____

_____

Chapter checklist:

	Good	Needs Work
Content		
1. Support of opinion with appropriate reasons and information	☐	☐
2. Level of interest of information	☐	☐
Organization		
1. Introduction, supporting paragraphs, and conclusion	☐	☐
2. Clear focus on topic	☐	☐
3. Use of examples to support reasons	☐	☐
Cohesion and style		
1. Use of transition sentences to introduce examples	☐	☐
2. Use of quotations	☐	☐
3. Use of adjective clauses	☐	☐

Difficulties with grammar to work on:

_____

_____

_____

Difficulties with form to work on:

_____

_____

_____

CHAPTER 11 FEEDBACK SHEET

Student Name _____ Date _____

Personal reaction:

_____

_____

_____

_____

_____

Chapter checklist:

	Good	Needs Work
Content		
1. Inclusion of facts, not opinions	☐	☐
2. Level of interest of title	☐	☐
Organization		
Answering questions "who?" "what?" "where?" "when?" and "why?"	☐	☐
Cohesion and style		
1. Use of adjective clauses	☐	☐
2. Omission of unnecessary words	☐	☐

Difficulties with grammar to work on:

_____

_____

_____

Difficulties with form to work on:

_____

_____

_____

CHAPTER 12 FEEDBACK SHEET

Student Name _____ Date _____

Personal reaction:

_____

_____

_____

_____

Chapter checklist:

	Good	Needs Work
Content		
1. Clarity of proposal	☐	☐
2. Use of supporting reasons	☐	☐
Organization		
1. Introductory paragraph	☐	☐
2. Conclusion	☐	☐
3. Arguments	☐	☐
4. Counterarguments	☐	☐
Cohesion and style		
1. Use of transition words linking paragraphs	☐	☐
2. Use of connecting words showing cause, result, and contrast	☐	☐
3. Use of conditional mood	☐	☐

Difficulties with grammar to work on:

_____

_____

Difficulties with form to work on:

_____

_____